Turn the Page

Patricia Piña

"Darle Vuelta a la Página"

2011, Patricia Piña Piñero

Spanish Edition

"Turn the Page"

2012, Patricia Piña Piñero

English Edition

malabarymedio@gmail.com

English Translation : Mónica León Aveleyra

To my husband, my daughter and my son;

Thank you for your love and support

Chapter 1

On one hand I felt sad, but on the other I felt relieved. My father had passed away and finally, he was in peace. His life had been a permanent struggle against an anxiety that he simply had not been able to control.

It had been ten years since my last visit to the huge old house at Xalapeños Ilustres Street but on this occasion the visit was unavoidable.

I traveled by car from Patzcuaro[1] to Mexico City. There I would meet my brother and mother at the airport in order to make the journey by bus to Xalapa together. Mexico City didn't give us a break and the rush hour made me remember one of the many reasons why my husband and I decided to leave the city: The traffic. It had taken us three long hours to cross the city from the Toluca highway to the city airport.

I had to meet my mother at eight pm at the international arrivals gate, because my

---

[1] Patzcuaro is a beautiful city in the state of Michoacán, Mexico.

brother was arriving from London at nine. My mother is extremely punctual (as am I) so by quarter past eight she was calling me on my cell phone.

- Hey, what happened? Where are you?
- Mami I'm close to the airport but we couldn't get there the usual way because there is some kind of construction work going on. It has taken us two hours through the traffic to cross the city, but we are on our way.

Bernardo tried another road. We thought that maybe through the new terminal (terminal 2) there might be some kind of new road to get to terminal one.

I got out of the car in order to ask for information at the Areomexico desk but the lady told me that if I didn't have a boarding pass it was not possible to get to terminal one. You had to go by car.

We took another route and were almost there when we found out that the road was closed and we couldn't turn around. My cell started to ring every five minutes.

- What happened? Where are you? It's almost nine and your brother is about to arrive!
- Mami, we are stuck in traffic but I'll be there any minute.

Twenty minutes later the car hadn't moved. It was amazing, there was no way to get to terminal one.

- Ok, I'm going to walk. – I suggested to Bernardo.
- Paty, don't even think about it! It's a very dangerous neighborhood! I'm not going to leave you here alone at this hour of the night. Sorry, they'll have to wait- he told me.

Another call.

- Sweetheart. Your brother has already arrived. I'm here with him. But where are you?
- Almost there... I hope. Why don't you guys get dinner in some restaurant at the airport and I'll meet you there.

Fifteen minutes later we finally arrived at terminal one.

My mother and my brother were sitting at the restaurant, given my lateness, and thanks to the remodeling of the road and the wonderful traffic signing system I was three hours late. Amazing! It takes three hours to get from Morelia to Mexico City[2], almost the same to cross the city! Anyway I was finally there. My husband Bernardo, my son Juan Maria and I had a light dinner. Then Bernardo and Juan Ma took us to the bus station where my mother, my brother, and I would continue our journey. I kissed Bernardo and Juan Ma goodbye and got on the eleven pm bus to Xalapa where we would arrive at three o'clock in the morning. The next day was going to be a long one so we took things easy.

We woke up and had breakfast at "Café La Parroquia"[3] I asked for a "lechero" and chicken "panuchos"[4]. As could be expected, at the restaurant my mother ran into some people

---

[2] Morelia is a city in Michoacán, a whole other state.

[3] Café La Parroquia is a very famous restaurant and an icon of the port of Veracruz in Mexico.

[4] "Lechero" is a drink of coffee with milk, "panuchos" are these puffy stuffed corn tortillas. In this case, stuffed with chicken.

she knew which gave us their condolences on my father's passing away.

I don't know what my mother's thoughts were on in those moments. She had been separated from my father for twenty five years and they had not spoken to each other in ten years, but they had still shared fifteen years of their lives and they had had a son and a daughter together. Mother was sad.

After breakfast we went to see my grandma "Yaya", my father's mother. I was nervous to go into that house and see her. Almost twelve years had passed since the last time I had spoken to her and I was scared to death to see my aunt "Charo" because I thought that she would yell at me. There had been some friction with my aunts because of my father alcoholism and the terrible things he had done because of it.

At the Xalapeños Ilustres house everything was the same. Time has stood still. To both sides of the main gate were the same shops. To the left side there was the "Cristal" Bookshop and to the right the Mercery Shop. In the sidewalk in front of it, there was this delicious "Dauzón" Bakery.

Very cordially, "Don Chon" welcomed me. His thin, tall silhouette and those facial features which didn't reveal his age had made time stop. He was one of those people who always look old.

- Good Morning, how are you? – he asked me.
- Very well Don Chon. Not to bad, given the situation.

I crossed the garage and walked though the central courtyard of the house, where, at the end, the 56 black Buick and the brown Galaxy were still parked. To the right was the old staircase that led to the second floor, where the actual living quarters where. How I loved those stairs! I said to myself. To walk up those half spiral "barro"[5] stairs with their wooden banister transported me immediately to the beginning of the twentieth century and made me imagine, at least for a moment, the time when the house was built. At the end of the stairs was the carved wooden door with an inscription at the top that read "1911". It was the main access to the inhabited part of the house. I loved it! To

---

[5] "Barro is a very popular material in Mexico. It is a kind of hardened mud or clay.

my back, in the corner, guarding the entrance and hiding the treasures which we dreamed were hidden somewhere in the house, was the image of the Virgen de Guadalupe[6].

I took a big breath before opening the wooden door. How many experiences I had lived through in that house! And in the end the house itself seemed suspicious, as if jealously hiding the secrets of the family within its depths.

It was amazing! Everything was in the same place, although the passing of time was evident. The wooden table with the marble slab on top, where the classic black phone seemed to wait for someone to call. In the corner my cousin's big dollhouse which all the younger cousins had used to dream of playing with, though it was strictly forbidden. All you could do was look at it and imagine all the adventures that went on inside. I couldn't′ resist the temptation to turn towards it, standing on it's swivel base, and look at it again. How many hours I had spent admiring it as a child! But time does not pass anything by. The dollhouse

6 Mexico's most celebrated Roman Catholic icon of the Virgin Mary.

was dusty and empty. Only my mind housed the memory of what it used to be, and the same was true of my grandmother's house.

I walked passed the hallway and to the first door to the right: The room, which had been my father's study. I looked in and found it, like the dollhouse, dusty and empty. For a moment I remembered him. I saw him behind his desk making his daily calls to me, to my brother, to his sisters... he used to call me every day to ask about the international price of coffee and somehow he would always steer the conversation into making me ask inevitable question: "How are you?"

Followed always by the same answer. "I could be better". I can't remember a single occasion in which he answered that he was ok. As for the coffee, the only part I shared in it was telling him the price. There wasn't anything else to share. Only once did I visit the coffee plantation he owned in Xalapa. For him I was just a woman so "what would I know about those things?"

Next door to his study was his room... Strange. It was empty, dusty and abandoned too but everything was the same. His bed, his bureau, his closet. In my mind I could still see his plastic flip-flops and his brown suede boots under the bed. His room communicated through an internal door with the last room of the hallway and when I crossed it I was overwhelmed by the same sensation: the house made its age felt.

It had withstood the passing of centuries, the passing of generations, the passing of life, but now it looked weak, tired, old. The happiness of the old times was gone and only the memories of what it had been for me, and the moments I had lived there, remained.

And there she was. Sitting on the couch of the small living room. Her beautiful blue eyes looked at me. "My dear Yaya". I hugged her and filled her face with kisses.

She burst into tears. So did I. I had missed her so much.

My father had passed away.

Suddenly, I put myself on guard. The voice was unmistakable.

- Isha. What a nice surprise! I'm very glad to see you. Victor, Berta. I gulped. It was my aunt Charo, and she acted as if nothing had ever happened. She welcomed us with the same love that she used to have for us.

- But please, sit down. Do you want something to drink? We have Coke, water, coffee?
- No, thank you, we just ate breakfast.
- Let me tell you, we had just visited Victor (my father) a week ago at the rehabilitation clinic at Coatepec and we talked with him. He was very fat, but I never imagined that this would happen - She continued telling us -On Tuesday the nurse phoned and told us that he had passed away. She mentioned that after lunch he went to take a nap as he always did, as we all do, but he didn't wake up. At that moment they contacted us. We tried to reach you but all your phone numbers are different from the ones I had. I suddenly remembered Edith, your friend, Berta, and I thought to myself - I'm sure she has Berta's phone number. And so she did! - Come on - She told us - Here in the chapel are his ashes, so you can see them.

My mother, my brother and I looked at each other. I don't think any of us knew what to say or do. I listened to my aunt Charo while I kept hugging my grandma Yaya.

- Yes, come on- She insisted.

Very obediently, we stood up and walked to the end of the corridor where the "chapel" was. It was really a small room next to the formal living room. Inside was a small altar. On one side stood a statue of Saint Joseph and on the other a statue of the Virgin Mary. Four candles were lit and right in the middle was a silver box with my father's ashes inside. In front of the altar were two *Prie Dieus*. We knelt down to pray for a moment and after that we returned where my Yaya was.

- Well, there he is, said Charo. He looked in peace and I'm very glad that we can turn the page.

- Hello, hello. What a surprise! Hi Patricia, Berta, hi Victor.

It was my aunt Graciela, she had just arrived, overwhelmed over everything she had to do. She always has a lot to do and she is always overwhelmed about everything. She looked the same as I remembered her.

Small, thin, her hair very well done. She was dressed in an angora sweater, skirt, tights, and heels.

- Don't go, we are almost ready to have lunch. - said Charo.

- Impossible, I have to go - said Graciela -I have to go to the bank, arrange the church papers and handle all the arrangements for the mass. Do you know? -She looked at us - Your father's mass is at seven o'clock this evening.

- Yes, we knew - My mother answered.

- Good. Well, I'm leaving and I'll see you tonight.

- And now tell me Ishilina, I heard that you live in Pátzcuaro? How is that possible!? - my aunt Charo asked me.

- That's the way it is -I didn't feel like explaining all the reasons that had led us to that decision after living in Mexico City for eight years. Also, in my heart I knew that she was not going to listen anyway. A talk with her is always a monologue where she is the only speaker.

My aunt is a big woman in every way. She is one of those people whose presence is felt the minute she steps in, and she likes to be the center of attention. She had been a great high school principal, a great friend, and everybody in Xalapa knows her. Although she's not tall, she is big. Dark brown hair, small brown eyes, ample nose, big breasts, big bottom and big legs. Always made up and well dressed, with a different style from that of my aunt Graciela, who is much more conservative, but also well dressed, although on this occasion she was wearing a sports outfit. When I see her it comes to my mind that some place in my genealogical tree there must be some African ascendant because of my aunt's appearance. I always loved her, but the problems that arose between her and my father made me distance myself from all my relatives that live in Xalapa.

We went to the dining room. It was a beautiful place. The table was huge. Twenty people could sit around it. As usual my aunt Charo sat at the head. To her right, my grandmother. My great aunt used to sit to her left but she passed away and now my brother sat in her place. I sat down next to my grandmother and my mother next to me. The lunch was delicious. Carrot soup, *cecina* (a kind of meat), black beans, white rice, green hot sauce, tortillas... At the table the only person that spoke was Charo. We all listened to her, the only thing that we could do was to make approving or disapproving noises.

When we were done, my aunt went to take a nap and we said goodbye to my grandmother. We went to the hotel to rest. I felt dazed.

Chapter 2

How many things I had lived through in that house! My childhood summer vacations had been spent in Xalapa. We lived in Mexico City and for vacations we would come here to visit my grandparents on my mothers side and on my fathers as well.

I remember that we always stayed at my mother's parents house. Mario was my grandfather and María de los Angeles was my grandmother, and we always called her "Lala". It would take us five long hours to get from Mexico City to Xalapa. It was exciting when we passed through Puebla on our way to Rio Frio in order to get to Perote, and on sometimes we would stop there to have lunch at a place called "La Covadonga", a small restaurant where you can find the best egg and chorizo *tortas*[7] that you can eat. At the corner there was a store where we would buy homemade candies

---

[7] Chorizo is a kind of pork sausage. Tortas a very popular Mexican sandwiches, made with specific kinds of bread.

known as *jamoncillo* and *chiles chipotles*[8]. Perote was an hour away from Xalapa.

That part of the road was a curvy slope that, on many occasions, was covered in mist.

- Are we almost there? -My brother and I asked.

- Almost there - Answered my mom.

- Almost... ¿how much?

- A few minutes.

Just when the whole family was starting to run out of patience, like magic, we would see the city lights through the mountains.

- Look, there's Xalapa! -My mother would cheer.

Time seemed to grow shorter as we saw the lights get closer and closer. Luckily my grandparent's house was very close to the entrance of the city so it would only take us only five minutes to get there.

My grandmother Lala always welcomed us at front garden and we would see her as we

---

[8] Chile Chipotle is a kind of chili pepper, very popular in Mexico.

were approaching the house. When I was a kid I never thought about how long she stood there waiting for us. In my mind she always went outside just in time.

- Hello my prince - She greeted my brother.

- Hello my princess - She greeted me - I'm so happy you are here! Come in. Your grandpa is waiting for you. Just in time!

Mario, my grandpa, was a man of habit. He would wait for us at a small bar that was inside the house. I don't remember what he offered my parents to drink, but for us it was always a small glass half full of *rompope*[9], not enough for me. I always wanted a little bit more, but I knew that was not possible so with my tongue I tried to reach every last drop of *rompope*.

One o'clock.

- Well mami. Is lunch ready? - My grandfather asked Lala.

- Papi, its almost ready, they are heating up the soup.

---

[9] Rompope is an eggnog-like drink made with eggs, milk and vanilla flavoring

- Ok, then we can go and sit down at the table.

- Papi, give us a few more minutes. We are very happy with Bertita and the kids.   They just arrived.

A few more minutes were a very difficult thing for my grandpa to grant. Two more minutes and that was it, we were walking into the dining room. A beautiful round table was waiting for us. There were six places perfectly set up. My grandfather sat with his back to a big window that overlooked the garage. To his right sat my grandmother, to his left my mother, I guess my father sat next to her but I don't remember clearly and in the other places were my brother's and mine.

My grandma rang a small bell that was kept next to her place at the table.

- The soup please. At that moment, Paula, the maid, entered through the door that connected the kitchen with the dinning room pushing a service cart on top of which came the soup bowl.

Lala served the plates and passed them until yours reached your place.

Yummy... I thought. It's alphabet soup. I loved that soup. I had fun trying to find my name or any other word in every spoonful.

- Ayyyyyy!!!! It's boiling! - I wailed after swallowing the first spoonful. My whole tongue was a big blister and I didn't want to think of what was happening to my throat. I felt how the soup burned its way through my esophagus and into the pit of my stomach. -It's boiling! - Why my grandma had the habit of serving soup at a boiling temperature is something I have never understood. I always tried to tell her that soup was heated enough when bubbles started to appear on the edge of the pot, but she would answer me:

- No, it's not ready. You have to wait until the bubbles are everywhere.

Of course, I thought, by that point the soup would be so hot that I would have to spend the next twenty minutes moving it with the spoon and blowing on it until I could put it in my mouth without burning it. Or, as in this case, I would forget this habit of my grandma's and burn my mouth.

The small bell sounded again.

- Can you bring the next course? Asked Lala.

Again, Paula entered. On the service cart she put the soup plates and went to the kitchen. Hurrying up she was back with two new platters on it. The first one contained white rice and the other, a stew.

- Bertita - Lala said to my mother - I cooked that stew you like so much.

- Yummy - said my mother - you shouldn't have bothered.

I simply couldn't believe it. I had already burnt my mouth with the soup and now here was that very hot, spicy stew that my mother loved. Of course, everybody ate a lot of hot chili and they enjoyed it, but I hadn't developed that habit.

- Princess - grandma said to me- let me have your plate.

- No, thank you, Lala. I only want some rice, the stew is a little bit hot for me.

- Don't be silly, come on! It's not that hot. I made it very mild because I knew you were coming. I'm just going to give you a little. You can take off the sauce and only eat the meat. My grandma explained lovingly to me.

I had no choice -Ok, just a little. - I told her.

My plate was on my place and it was time to start eating. A little rice and a little bit of stew with no sauce. One, two, three - I said to myself. I held my breath and put the food in my mouth, but I couldn't swallow it. It was stuck in my throat and I started to choke. What a scene! At this point the hot meat touched my burnt tongue and I finally swallowed it. Immediately I started to sweat and my nose started to run. This stew was very hot!

When they saw that I was sweating, with a runny nose, my face red and not precisely because of the weather, my grandma rang the bell again and said:

- Paula, come here please.

Paula looked at me with a mocking smile on her face.

- Yes, ma'am -Paula said.

- See if you can rinse Patricia's meat, she says it is too hot for her even without sauce.

Five minutes later, Paula was back with my rinsed meat. It was horrible. Finally with the help of half a gallon of lemonade I ate it. I knew what my favorite part of the meal was: Dessert. For dessert we were having *mantecado.* It's a vanilla homemade ice cream. It was delicious! My brother and I always asked for more until we finished it. My grandma only made a small container, so you always wanted a little bit more.

My grandpa started to tell us his childhood stories while grandma drank a cup of coffee. After his parents died, my grandpa and his five brothers were left to the care of his only older sister, Maria de la Salud. She was fifteen and my grandpa was about eight. Now that I'm a grown up I regret not having paid more attention to my grandpa's stories. There are so many things that I would like to ask him now! But when you are eight years old, the only thing that matters is to be able to leave the table and go play. We were not allowed to excuse ourselves from the table until my grandpa was over, so time passed very slowly for me during those meals.

Chapter 3

Holidays went by peacefully. Most of the time we were at grandpa's house. The only outings were to the supermarket or to go to dinner at Yaya´s house.

On my mom's side of the family I had two girl cousins and three boy cousins. Later on I found out about five more cousins that I didn't know of. My girl cousins had a distant relationship with my grandparents so I almost never saw them. The only one that visited them was my cousin Jaime and since he was a boy, well, he played with my brother. They played a game similar to tennis that they had invented in the back patio of the house. They divided the patio in two with a rope that they tied to two chairs, one on each side. Racquets were substituted by their own hands and the ball actually was a tennis ball. They had a great time! I waited sometimes for hours until their match was over and I could have the chance to play, but they played a rematch over and over again, until I bored of waiting my turn and went inside to play dolls by myself instead.

Sometimes I made puzzles or drew. But sometimes my imagination waned and I felt bored.

At that point I would go to the kitchen to see what they were cooking for lunch, hoping that there where no plans for hot stews.

I liked it very much when they made *tortillas* . They would buy the corn dough and hand make tortillas. Two maids helped my grandmother. The first one was in charge of cleaning the second floor of the house and of the laundry. The second one was in charge of the first floor and the kitchen, but when they made *tortillas* both of them helped. Thanks to them and to their patience I learned to make *tortillas*.

The first *tortilla* that I made was more like a *gordita* (a kind of fat tortilla) I couldn't flatten the ball of corn enough to make it a *tortilla*. And it was not well cooked because I turned it over on the *comal* (a kind of flat pan) so many times that it turned out uncooked on the inside and toasted on the outside.

- What a delicious *gordita* you made! -Paula told me with love.

- If you want to make a tortilla, you have to do the same thing but you need to hit it with your palm a little bit harder.

I got it and did it that way, but it didn't work out. The mass was smeared all over the round plastic that we used to make the tortillas. It was a disaster.

- You are hitting too hard. Be patient.

Finally, I made a tortilla. I managed to separate the flattened mass from the plastic without breaking it and put it on the *comal* to cook. What I didn't manage to do was turn it over in time. It took me too long so it got dry and turned to toast. Horrible!

- You are doing very well - Paula cheered me on - I didn't explain to you that when you put the *tortilla* on the *comal* you have to wait only until the edge turns a little bit white, and that is the first time you need to turn it over. The second time is when some small brown spots start to appear underneath and the last time is when the tortilla fluffs up and a bigger brown spot appears underneath. If you turn it over more times the tortilla will toast and burn and if you don't turn it over enough times the *tortilla* will be raw.

As everything in life, things have a way of getting done and you have to turn over the tortilla at the right time in order for it to be done correctly. I felt very proud when after many *tortilla* failures I finally got it right. It was the best *tortilla* I have ever eaten.

Another day, Lala invited me to the kitchen so I could learn to season black beans. I remember that on the stove there was a pot with mashed beans on it. She was stirring them with a wooden spoon.

- Taste this- Lala told me as she put a small amount of beans on my hand.

- As you can see, they are not so tasty and it's because they need salt and seasoning. She put some salt on them and stirred again. Five minutes later she took my hand again and placed a small amount of beans on it. Taste them - she told me. What do you think?

- They are very good. - I said.

- They taste different, don't you think? But they still need a little bit of salt. She repeated the same procedure as before and made me taste again.

- What do you think?

- They are delicious. Now they taste like your beans always do.

That is how during the holidays and thanks to my lack of cousins I learned to cook the way my grandmother did. By tasting and detecting the difference between flavors that results from adding some ingredients to food. I loved it! I always shared this joy for cooking with her.

At Lala´s home it was an odyssey to go to the supermarket. We had to take a cab that took us downtown where you could find the only supermarket in town: "Chedraui". It was not very nice. The aisles where narrow, it had two floors and no electric stairs, sometimes the articles you needed were on the second floor so you had to leave your grocery cart, go upstairs, try to carry what you needed and go downstairs to put it in the cart. For me, the second floor had a special interest: Toys. And sometimes grandma would buy me one.

The store only had five checkout lines and we didn't have the bar code system. So the cashier registered prices item by item on the cash register in order to calculate the final sum.

Finally a *cerillo*[10] would help us put the groceries in bags, put the bags in another cart, hail a taxi, and put the bags in the trunk. It was not easy to get a taxi. Sometimes grandma asked the kid to walk up two or three blocks to ask a taxi to pick us up at the store entrance. There were no parking spaces so when a taxi finally stopped, the kid would help us put all the bags in the trunk while all the cars honked their horns so we would hurry up. Grandma would then give the kid a tip and tell the taxi the home address. It was a mystery to me why we had to bother this much because of a grocery issue. My grand pa was the owner of coffee plantations and a coffee processing plant that was next to the house. There he had cars, trucks, and a chauffeur that could easily have given us a ride to the supermarket. But that never happened.

In those days there were products that you could only find in Mexico City. They were not distributed to other cities in Mexico. Lala would always ask my mother to take her certain things like Tetra Pak milk cartons, multigrain packaged bread, certain candies, etc.

---

[10] A teenagers that help you put your groceries into bags.

As I said before, my grandfather was the owner of two coffee plantations and a coffee processing plant. The plantations names were "Cerro Gordo" and "Plan de las Hayas". The processing plant was next to my grandparent's house in Xalapa. I never visited the processing plant. The only part that I knew was the outside that I could see from the back patio of the house. What would I know of those things! I was a woman! That's the way my grandfather and my father felt about certain issues. The only place I was allowed to visit was my grandpa's office and it seemed to me that my grandma had to make an appointment so that we could visit him.

The building was like a "shoe box". At the entrance there was a big wooden counter. In the first section you could see the accountant's desk and my grandpa's secretary's desk. It was the administrative area. At the end was my grandpa's office. I visited him there three or four times in my whole life. We only went there when Lala told us to. She would say "Why don't you go to grandpa's office to give him a kiss?" That was the only time when my brother and I would dare to cross the forbidden line between the office and the house.

When we got there, Lupita, the secretary, would greet us happily.

- Hi, what a nice surprise, I'm glad to see you! It's kind of a miracle that you are here!

- Hi - we would say in shy voices.

- Come in. Let me see if you can visit Don Mario.

- Don Mario - We could hear at the distance - Your grandchildren are here to visit you. Can they come in?

- Tell them to come in - My grandpa would reply.

Lupita would approach us - He said you can come in.

- Hi grandpa- My brother and I said to him in unison. Grandpa would lean over and give each of us a kiss on the forehead. I don't remember the few phrases that we would exchange. Five minutes later we were back with Lupita. She would give us a lollypop that we would eat on our way back home.

I never knew the "Plan de las Hayas" plantation. My mom says it was too far away. She told us that it was a very big plantation.

There were mainly coffee plants but there were also mango and orange trees.

"Cerro Gordo" plantation was half an hour from Xalapa on the highway from Xalapa to Veracruz. Sometimes we went there. My mother told me that "Cerro Gordo" was my grandpa's hobby, he loved to go there every Saturday morning and visit the coffee plants and the mango and orange trees. He didn't get a profit from this place but he really enjoyed it, and so did we. The coffee was not so good, the one that he got at "Plan de las Hayas" was better, because the land was at a higher altitude and it was colder.

Every time we wanted to go to "Cerro Gordo" we had to convince my grandmother and my mother. Sometimes their excuse for not going was that they knew there was a *Norte* (strong winds) in Veracruz and it was very probable that it would be raining. Other times they said we could go but the pool was empty and on other occasions there were no explanations at all. When we woke up my grandpa had already left to "Cerro Gordo" and lunch had to be ready at one o'clock so it was not possible for us to go. Grandpa never invited us to go with him to "Cerro Gordo". At the time that never struck me as odd. That was just the way things were.

But when we did manage to go to "Cerro Gordo" it was very exciting. The night before they would tell us that we were going and that grandpa had had a talk with the local people and gotten permission to fill the pool with water. We would get up early in the morning to get together everything we needed: A change of clothes, a bathing suit, a towel, etc. My mother and Lala would take care of the food, usually *pambazos* with ham and black beans.

When we finally got there, we would change as quickly as we could and head to the pool. It was very deep. Only the steps where shallow. I enjoyed swimming from one end of the pool to the other but it was very deep so when I got tired I had to go to the edge and rest. At the pool's edge there was a water channel where toads liked to sit and rest. More than once I was horrified by the feeling of a spongy, slimy creature brushing my hand. When that happened my tiredness disappeared and I swam as fast as I could towards the pool steps.

- In fifteen minutes we are having lunch - Lala would tell us.

- Nooooo - We shouted. What time is it?

- It's almost one o´clock and grandpa is on his way.

- Ahhhh - We lamented. We didn't want to get out.

Lunch was very simple. Toasted tortillas with black beans, lettuce, and cheese on them. *Pambazos* that are these kind of small rolls with ham, beans, lettuce and tomatoes inside. Lemonade, and if it was the right season, mangos.

After lunch we had to wait half an hour to get back in the pool because lunch had to be digested. We always tried to negotiate a few minutes but we never succeeded.

- No - Said Lala- If you swim now you will have indigestion.

And so because of that fear... we waited.

Those days always seemed very short because we always had to go back to Xalapa at six o'clock so dinner would be ready at seven. My grandpa demanded that and made no concessions. The exception was Christmas day, when dinner was at nine.

What a pity that my children didn't get to know these places that I enjoyed in my childhood! The 1987 Mexican crash and the economic crisis led my grandparents (at the age of seventy) to lose everything and end up living in a small rented apartment in Mexico City for the rest of their lives.

Chapter 4

In Yaya´s house things were very different. The routine was much more relaxed. She lived in a big old house downtown and in that same house lived her sister (my aunt Ceci), my aunt Charo, and her kids, Charito and Armando. My grandfather died of a heart attack when my father was fifteen and he never talked about him, as if he had erased any memories he had about him. The few things I know about him are that he was a high school history teacher and that at some point in his life, they offered him a job at the Mexican Train Company in Mexico City. So he went to live there but my father and his older sister stayed at the house in Xalapa with their grandparents while two younger sisters went with them to Mexico City. While living there he had the heart attack and died so my father never saw him again. Perhaps that was when his problems began. It was funny but when I asked my grandmother about Victor Gustavo, my grandfather, she would give me the same answer that my father gave me, that she didn't remember anything. As for my father, the only thing he would add was that he had never understood why they had left him and his older sister in Xalapa. Who knows.

In Mexico we use both parent's last names. We usually write down our first name and then our two last names: First the father's and then the mother's. My last names have always been the cause of much laughter and disbelief because in Spanish they are like a word game.

- What's your name? - How many times are you asked that question in a lifetime for one reason or another? Thousands!

- Patricia - I respond.

- And your last names?

- Piña Piñero

-Piña what? Almost on every occasion they ask me again.

- Piñero - I respond again.

The other person looks at me like he or she doesn't understand why I'm playing a joke on him/her when it's a simple question.

- Excuse me? He/She asks again.

- Piñero - I respond. After so many times of having been asked the same question repeatedly, now is the time when I make my joke:

- Do you know apples?

- Yes? - They respond.

- It's like the apple tree, but instead of apples think of pineapples.[11]

With a smile on his/her face he/she tells me - Come on, you have to be kidding!

- No, I'm not. I cannot be more serious about it. Those are my last names and I assure you that if my parents had tried to achieve this they probably wouldn't have been able to pull it off. But they did.

Even though my last names are very similar, my parent's family's stories are very different.

Unlike my mother's family, my father's family had formal education. My grandmother and her sister were the first women to get

---

[11] In Spanish it's a word game. Manzana- manzanero. Piña -Piñero

Bachelor's degrees in Chemistry and Bio-pharmaceutical Chemistry at the National University (UNAM) in Mexico City. My grandmother tells the story of how her father pushed her to go to Mexico City to study with her sister because her sister couldn't go by herself, so they both went. She obeyed her father and got her degree and then they returned home to Xalapa. In those times that was very unusual. After that they both taught at Xalapa's high school until they retired. My aunt Ceci was a chemistry teacher and all her students feared her, including her niece Maggie.

Chemistry was tough and my aunt Ceci was a strict teacher. For Maggie it was not an easy subject and she was failing. The final exam came and although she studied very hard, she failed. However, she had another opportunity to take the exam during the summer. The family was mad at Ceci, but she wasn't going to make any concessions to Maggie just because she was her niece. She had to study and pass the exam. Maggie cried but she knew there was no choice. She had to study a lot. Finally she passed and peace came back into the house. Aunt Ceci lived in that house since she was born, and so did my grandmother, but Ceci never got married and she always told people proudly that she was "Miss" Ceci. She was quite a character.

During many years of my childhood we would have Christmas dinner on the 24th at my maternal grandparents house and on the 25th we would eat lunch with my paternal grandmother. Yaya and aunt Ceci had dinner with us on the 24th. The ritual was the same every year.

Early in the morning of the 24th, we would eat breakfast. Immediately afterwards my brother would go play. I don't remember what my father would do, but us women would start to worry about preparing everything for the evening's dinner. Lala would set the most elegant tablecloth she had, the most beautiful set of silver cutlery. Cloth napkins at every place. At the center of the table was the place of the silver candlesticks with red candles. The kitchen was a battleground. On one hand lunch had to be ready at one o clock and on the other Christmas Eve dinner had to be ready by nine. The menu was:

- Sherry chicken broth

- Vizcaina codfish

- Stuffed turkey and mashed apples

- Dessert: "*Buñuelos de viento*" (A kind of fried pastry)

I entered in action at this point. I loved those *buñuelos*. My Lala always said that they were very laborious to make, so if I wanted some I had to help her. The recipe is easy with simple ingredients. The key is that you can't stop moving the batter with a wooden spoon until it reaches it's point. There are moments that you feel that you can't keep moving it, your arm starts to hurt. When I reached this point to my good fortune Lala would appear and with a fast movement take the spoon and continue moving the batter. The satisfaction of work well done was the moment that dessert was served at the table and I tasted those delicious *buñuelos de viento* that I had made.

Chapter 5

My father was an absent father. He was an alcoholic. He always felt sorry about it but he would constantly relapse into it. It was hard for me to understand him and I went through different stages. When I learned about his problem I was ten years old. Our family had just decided to move from Mexico City to Xalapa. For me the move was unexpected.

Every summer we went to Xalapa on vacations to visit the family and friends. We usually stayed at Lala´s house and we went to visit Yaya. But that summer vacations were a little bit longer than they used to be. Just a few days before school started my parents told us that we were moving to Xalapa. I was already enrolled for fifth grade at an elementary school called "*Las Hayas*" and my brother was going to attend middle school at a public school: *Secundaria Tecnica 3*. He had gotten into this school thanks to my aunt.

I was shocked. How this could be? I was not going to se my friends again? And what was going on here! They didn't explain anything about it to me. But the decision was made. We bought our school uniforms and books to go to school in Xalapa.

My aunt Graciela, my father's sister, was going to take me and pick me up from school. Her kids were going the same school as I was. My brother and I were going to stay at Yaya´s house while my parents made all the arrangements for the move.

For me all of this had the feel of an adventure, but I was scared of the first day of school. The school building was very simple. The classrooms consisted of an aluminum pre-fabricated construction that surrounded a central patio, but the landscape where it was built was beautiful. To get there we had to take the old Xalapa-Coatepec road for 4 miles then we took a detour that took us on a dirt road from which you could see farms and cornfields on both sides. My favorite days were those when you couldn't see farther than 30 inches away because of the fog and the humidity. This atmosphere made you feel nostalgic.

Once I went through the first difficult days of school I felt very happy there. It was fun when in the middle of history class a cow entered through the door. We all shouted and tried to make it return to the pasture. Physical Education class consisted of climbing the hill that was in front of the school and playing hide and seek there. The grass was so tall there that you could hide just by lying down. We had a lot of fun.

Unfortunately at home things were not the way they used to be. My parents rented a house in the suburbs in a place called *Las Animas*. The design of the house was curious to me because the living room, dining room, the kitchen, the guest bathroom and my parent's room were all on the first floor, while my room, another bathroom, and my brother's room were downstairs. We only used that bathroom to go to the toilet because for some reason we took our showers in my parent's bathroom.

The moving truck arrived with our things, but we never finished unpacking. The boxes with the things for the living room and dining room remained unpacked and the boxes with my parent's things were half unpacked. Only my brother and I decided to fix up our rooms.

My mother spent hours making expense lists: Rent, electric bill, phone bill, tuition, groceries, and added them together over and over.

My father got out of bed later and later every day. And then there came a time when he didn't get out of bed all day. He only came out of his room to get something to eat.

One night my mother called us. She wanted to have a talk with us. So we sat around the kitchen table. My father sat as if on a prisoner's dock.

- I want to tell you that your father has a problem- My mother said to us.

- That is why we are living in Xalapa, because your father is not well -She continued.

I knew things were not ok. (How perceptive!)

- Your father takes pills.

Pills? In my mind everything was all mixed up. At some point everybody takes a pill. When you have a headache or a stomachache. What's wrong with taking a pill! I didn't understand. Mom continued with her explanation.

- He also drinks alcohol.

Well, yes, I thought. I had seen grown-ups drinking a glass of wine or brandy, maybe tequila.

- And that is the reason we don't have money. He lost his company and now your grandmother gives us some money to pay the bills. Tell them Victor! Tell your kids what's going on! Mom was desperate. My dad didn't say a word, he just stared at the table.

Finally he said - What your mother is saying is true.

- I have a problem with drugs and alcohol.

- Well, I finally said. Everybody drinks and I love you very much. Don't you love us? Why you are doing this? - I asked him.

He didn't look at me. He only said. - I love you all very much, but I'm sick.

Sick? Sick with what? If you are sick go and see a doctor. He will give you a prescription, you will take the medicine, and that's it. I didn't understand. I was so immersed in my thoughts, and the strange thing is I have never spoken to my brother about what he was thinking in those moments. Probably something much more coherent than what I was thinking.

He was thirteen years old and I was just ten. Now that we are adults we never talk about this issue. It's still painful so we avoid it.

After this talk the family got sick. I cried, hidden in the service room that was above the kitchen and longed for the days when we were a "happy" family. My mom spent hours locked up in the guest bathroom with her cousin the psychologist. My dad didn't leave his room in days. The air inside it was sour and foul. My brother locked himself in his room and listened to music all day long. Nobody visited us.

Chapter 6

School was a kind of island of refuge. I had very good friends and I was very happy there. Some of my friend's families owned coffee plantations and they had birthday parties there. I particularly remember Rosa Aurora's birthday party. Her family owned "La Bola de Oro" coffee. The party took place in Coatepec´s coffee plantation. On the invitation they suggested you bring a change of clothes because it was possible that you would get wet. My mother drove me to Coatepec, a small town very close to Xalapa, and she had to pick me up at around seven at night.

The fun started when they showed us the green coffee bean warehouse. It was a huge warehouse where you could see three or four big coffee bean piles. They were around 13 feet tall. We started to feel more comfortable little by little. The first one to slide down the coffee mountain was Gonzalo, and we immediately followed his example. The feeling of sliding upside down with your arms open was fantastic.

Don Juan was in charge of the place and he was going to be our guide on our walk through the river. Wow! That really sounded incredible. Fifteen kids grabbed the rope. Don Juan was out in front with one end and another worker was at the back with the other one. We started the journey through the river. At some places the river was not deep, we only got our shoes wet, but suddenly it started to get deeper until the water reached our chest and the current was strong so we had to hold on to the rope tightly or lose our balance. We all got really wet.

When the river trip ended we went back to the main house. There we changed our clothes and got something for supper. Ham and bean pambazos (rolls) and a glass of milk. Then we went back home. It had been so much fun.

The school year went on. At home my parents asked us again and again what we preferred, to live here or to go back to México? I always answered to stay in Xalapa. I really liked it a lot. I had a lot of fun with my friends, I could visit my grandparents, my aunts and cousins. Of course sometimes I missed Mexico City. I missed going to the movies, because in those days there was only a theater in the city and the new releases took a long time to get to the towns. I missed my ballet lessons and my friends, but despite all of that I enjoyed living in Xalapa.

The truth is deep down my mother didn't like living in Xalapa. My father felt too much anxiety even thinking about going back and paying the bills over there. Mexico City was much more expensive.

My mother won. The next year we went back to Mexico. I went back to my old school but things had changed. They were different from a year ago. My friends were different. I felt completely out of place. I was tired of giving explanations about why I had gone away and why I was back. Besides, I was still thinking about playing yard games like jumping rope at recess and my friends were talking about their... boyfriends? But time softens everything and little by little I began to adapt.

I don't know exactly when everything happened, but we were preparing our sixth grade graduation. My life was in chaos. My parents couldn't stand each other. My mother was sleeping in one room, my father in another. Money was scarce. My friends were distant, or I had distanced myself from them, I was embarrassed to invite them over to my house and for them to see my father in the state he was in. There were times when he wouldn't leave his room for days at a time. I was worried and sometimes for no reason I wanted to go into his room to see how he was doing. Many times the door was locked and others his demeanor was regrettable. The room smelled of piss combined with vomit and stagnant air. It was very unpleasant and sad to see the state in which my father had ended up. What went on in his mind? Didn't he think about us? I loved him very much and I didn't understand what I had done for him to end up that way. The explanation I was given was that he was sick and that he should be treated as a sick person. It was very hard for me to understand that explanation and I couldn't treat him like a sick person because physically he was as strong as an ox, there was nothing wrong with him. Luckily, there was a time when he did leave his room. The period of abstinence was terrible, it was necessary to hide anything that had any, insignificant as it may have been, content of alcohol. Of course at home there where no spirits, wines, or beers. No alcohol even to heal with, because my father would drink it. No perfumes or lotions either, because he would drink those, too. Without noticing it, I finished elementary school.

How could I help? Maybe I could sell something so there would be a little more money at home, but what? Deep down I knew the only way I could help my family was to get good grades so they would at least not have to worry about paying for my tuition. What else could I do? I was 12 years old. There was no way I could bring money to the house, I didn't know what to do to make my father stop drinking, to make my mother at peace and happy.

On the day of my graduation I was happy, but sad at the same time. I didn't feel I was sharing a happy moment with my friends. What friends? I had pushed them away from me. Besides, at home a big effort had been made in order to purchase the tickets for the graduation dinner and mass. The dress I was wearing had been lent to me by a friend that had graduated a year earlier and it was too big for me at the chest, so I couldn't lean over without exposing myself and therefore I couldn't move freely.

My mother, so sweet and enthusiastic, had volunteered to be the group vocal, so she and two other moms were the organizers of the celebration. Incredibly, I cannot remember whether my father was present or not. Probably not. I think it is probable that the anxiety won over and he relapsed. Also, I think my mother probably preferred him to stay at home rather than make a spectacle of himself at the reception.

The mass was at the Pedregal Church. We were all very elegant and happy to have concluded a cycle of study. Later, the party would be celebrated in a hall in the Plaza de San Jacinto in San Angel. In one table sat my "friends" and I sat apart at another table, I don't remember with whom. At those moments I was thinking that I had finished elementary school. My grade average was 9.5 and that gave me the possibility to apply for a scholarship for junior high and relieve my parents of an economic burden, and that made me feel happy.

Chapter 7

September 19th, 1985. The worst alcoholic crisis had passed and the period of abstinence presented itself. My father resurged from the shadows. That day he showered, shaved, dressed, and left early in the morning with my mother for an important work appointment. It was the first time they lent my brother the car so he could drive us to school. So we had breakfast and then went out to the garage where Victor, my brother, asked me to open the garage door so he could pull out the red Caribe. As I headed towards the door I felt as though I had missed a step, then I felt dizzy, as if everything was moving. In fact, everything WAS moving.

- It's an earthquake! - I yelled at my brother. Instinctively we ran outside and held each other.

A few moments later everything was calm, the light cables slowly stopped moving.

- Whoa! -It had been a strong earthquake.
- Yes, it was strong -My brother said.

My brother pulled the car out of the garage, I closed the door, and we left for school. The situation in the south of the city was normal. We got there with no problems and at school everyone was commenting the issue.

- Did you feel the earthquake?
- Yes. It was strong - Said some.
- Was there an earthquake? - Others asked

During the first part of the morning everything elapsed normally. At around 10 am, when we were in recess, the principal's voice was heard on the loudspeaker:

"As many of you know, there was an earthquake in the city today and some buildings downtown collapsed. For this reason I ask those of you who brought cars to please go back home now. Those of you who didn't, please call home so they can pick you up. The telephone in the office is at your disposal." Of course in those times we didn't even imagine that some day everyone would have a phone in the pocket of his or her jeans.

We arrived home. My mother and father had not come back yet. We turned on the TV in order to try to understand what had happened. The TV channels that were working were those of the open TV: Channel 2, 4, 5, 11, and 13. Cablevision's service coverage was very limited and there was no Direct TV or Sky back then. That day we chose channel 2. Jacobo Zabludovsky[12] was on with a special transmission, narrating the events that had occurred in the center of the city. Several buildings had collapsed, there were hundreds of people missing, and the telephone service was failing.

The telephone rang.

- Hello? -I picked up.
- Hello! Are you all right?
- Yes, everything is fine. We came home because at school they asked us to.
- I heard on the radio that there was an earthquake and a lot of buildings fell down. What happened?
- I don't know exactly. Here everything is normal and on the news they are saying that too.
- Please don't leave the house. We're on our way.

---

[12] A famous newsperson in Mexico

At that moment I could not imagine the magnitude of the earthquake. Little by little we became aware of the havoc it had caused. So many buildings had collapsed, there were hundreds of deaths and hundreds of people missing.

Classes were suspended for two weeks. My school became a collection center. High school students, teachers, and directives organized themselves in brigades in order to take the food, water and other articles that people kindly brought to the shelter.

The next Monday we went to school in order to see how we could help. We were asked to take boiled eggs and purified water to the collection center that had been temporarily installed at the Humana Hospital (now the Angeles del Pedregal Hospital) because at school the brigades had already left to take the help to the disaster areas. Quickly my mother, my brother, and I made our way to a deposit in order to buy ten cartons of eggs and then to get some one liter glass bottles (Jumex juice) to sterilize and fill with drinkable water. In those days in Mexico there where no packaged water bottles. In some places they sold big glass water bottles, but they were expensive, heavy and not very practical for what was needed at that moment.

For the rest of that day, while the eggs boiled in a big pot that my mother had put over the fire, my brother and I washed the glass bottles. Once they were washed we put them in a pot of boiling water in order to sterilize them. Ten minutes later, we took them out, let them cool, and filled them with water that had been boiled, that is, purified water. Then we closed them and put them in a carton box so we could finally take them.

Then next day we took them to the Humana Hospital and there they asked us if we could take them ourselves. We didn't think twice about it. Of course!

- Where do we have to take them? -Asked my mother.

    - To a building that collapsed on Xola street.

We got in the car and headed there. As we got closer I realized more fully the magnitude of the disaster. Many streets were closed to traffic and many buildings looked damaged, but my real surprise was when we got to the address we had been given.

I could not believe my eyes. In the corner, over a great mountain of debris were the remains of a building whose floors had collapsed, one on top of the other. This couldn't be possible!

There were many people surrounding the building. People came and went, others were pulling debris out. Still others were just staring at the building, stunned. We couldn't find the collection center where we were supposed to leave the things we had brought.

From a distance a man yelled:

- You brought things for the collection center!
- Yes, eggs and drinkable water.
- Good! Please bring the water here and take the eggs to that blue canvas over there. His finger pointed the place out.

My mother and I stayed next to the water while my brother took the boiled eggs to the place the man had pointed out.

- Be silent! Please! Be silent! - A voice came from afar.

After a few seconds the crowd grew silent.

- Don't move and keep silent! They are trying to hear if there is anyone trapped in the debris! - The voice said again.

No one moved or spoke. It seemed as if for a moment time stood still. The only thing that could be heard were the steps of two people that followed two German Shepherds that sniffed among the debris. The minutes passed and the silence grew more and more dense. In the atmosphere you could feel everyone's hope that someone had survived. Nothing. The men moved slowly in the direction of the dogs sniffing... Nothing. One hour later, the searching stopped. The dogs had been unable to detect any movement. Nostalgically, time came back. We went back home.

All of those days everyone was very watchful of the news. On television they announced that there was to be no more taking supplies to the collection centers. There was more than enough to supply the shelters. The lists of missing people grew larger. The number of collapsed and damaged buildings also grew. In the ruins of the Juarez Hospital thirteen newborn babies were found alive, and the news filled us all with hope that more survivors would be found, but sadly, as the days passed, that hope faded.

Life began to normalize. School began again and we went back to our daily routine.

Chapter 8

The constant rise in prices made my parents permanently worried. At that time the inflation in Mexico rose to 63.75%, then in 1986 to 105% and in 1987 to 159% It was crazy! I remember that when she could, my mother would buy a little more of some products than was necessary because she knew that the next week they would cost more. Deodorants, toothpaste, toilet paper, canned tuna fish, marmalades, etc. Unfortunately, my family had been unable to buy a house, so just as the products became more expensive, so did rent, until there came a time when it was impossible for my parents to cover it in the house where we lived at that time.

My father got a job in Tijuana and went to live there. I don't know for certain, but I think that given his previous inconsistency at work and with his sobriety, we stayed in Mexico City.

- I need you to help me find a house. In three months we have to leave this one -

My mother said to my brother and I - So if you know of any apartment that one of your friends parents is renting, let me know. I have a little bit of money saved, but I have been checking the paper and the amount I have won't cover even a third of what an apartment costs in the Unidad Independencia.

I was very worried. I felt we had few options. We had to rent again. There was no way to ask for a mortgage and of course we didn't have enough to buy a house. At the time I was fifteen and I had moved six times.

My brother is three years older. I think he was worried too, so he tried to look for a way to create a business that would help the family. He tried to sell coffee, but quality coffee wasn't very appreciated then, so what he made out of it he practically had to use to pay for the transportation of the coffee from Coatepec to Mexico City. Later he learned that if you bought a baby cow, raised it, and later sold it, you could make a good profit out of the deal, so he pooled his money and bought the cow, but he needed a piece of land where the cow could graze and grow. He started to look for a place and at the same time he would write down phone numbers of apartments and houses where we could move. One day it occurred to him that it would be a good idea to look through the Ajusco area since there were larger pieces of land there than those to be found in the city. That night he told my mother and me:

- Something strange happened to me today. I was on my way to the Ajusco and I went through some streets that are beyond Reino Aventura (Six Flags today)[13] to see if I could find a piece of land for the cow. I covered several streets and I couldn't find anything. Then I saw a peasant that was resting leaning against a tree. His face was bowed and a big hat was covering his face, so I approached him and said:
- Good afternoon. Excuse me, I have a small cow and I was wondering if you might know of some piece of land where someone could take care of it for me - Without looking up, he lifted his arm and pointed towards a right corner and said:
- They are selling a house over there. Why don't you go ask?

---

[13] Reino Aventura was an amusement park and it became Six Flags.

- No, look- I said -I don't want a house, I'm looking for a small piece of land.
- Right- he said again without looking up - there's a house there. Go and ask.
- I wasn't getting anywhere with him -my brother told us- so I thanked him and got in the car, but then I thought, why not? I'll go to that house the man told me about. At the entrance there was a carton sign that said "To sell". I rang the bell and a man answered the door.
- Good afternoon.
- Good afternoon.
- I'm looking for a piece of land where someone can take care of a small calf and that peasant over there told me to ask here.
- How strange -The man said - Because I couldn't look after a calf here. I'm selling the house because we are going to live outside the city, but since you're here, why don't you take a look.

So I went in, my brother told us. It was a very strange house, because in the middle of what appeared to be a garage for two cars, there are three or four pine trees in a row. The house is yellow on the outside. When you go in there is a small living room, you go through another door and you enter a big living room where in the corner there is a small bar with two stools. Towards the center of the room there is a hallway that leads to the dining room on the left and to the kitchen on the right, and straight ahead there are two big rooms. There is bathroom with no sink and next to the living room there is a half bathroom. It's very strange but, guess what?! He turned toward my mother. I asked him how much he was asking for it and he said twenty five million pesos (in that time they had not taken 3 zeros off the peso and everything was in thousands and millions) and I remembered you told us that you had twenty millions saved. Look mom, it's not a pretty house, it's very strange, but why don't we go see it?

My mother didn't think twice about it. We went to see it. The description that my brother had given us was very accurate. It wasn't a pretty house, but it could be ours. Besides, with some paint it could look better.

We didn't have enough. We were five million pesos short. What could we do? For some reason I remembered my mother had some jewelry that she could sell and I told her:

-   Hey mom, what if you sell your jewelry?

- Well yes, of course, but I have no idea who would buy them.
- Well I don't know, maybe one of your friends.

My mother had some friends who were in comfortable economic positions, so maybe one them could buy them.

She offered them the jewelry but they only bought a ring and a bracelet. Between both, she had only raised one million, we were four millions short. Time passed and the date when we would have to leave the house we were living in was closer and we still had no other option. We had to get the money! My mother went to some places where they offered to buy things like watches and gold, but the prices they offered were an insult. It wasn't worth it and it didn't solve our problem.

- Mom, what if you offer the rings and the watch to the owner of the house as the rest of the payment? It occurred to me one night while we were having dinner.
- I don't think he'll want them- she said.
- Tell him anyway, the worst that can happen is he'll say no.
- Well I'll try.

So the three of us went to see the man with the jewelry and my mother made her offer. To our surprise, the man agreed. When he saw my mother's jewelry, his eyes opened wide and shone and he said he agreed.

- Only when we sign the contract, a jewelry appraiser has to see them in order to guarantee that it is good jewelry- said the man.
- Of course - answered my mother- No problem.

A date was set to give an advance on the money, appraise the jewelry, and sign the contract. For the peace of mind of both parties, the operation would take place in the office of a notary that was friends with the owner of the house.

My mother was nervous, but she had no choice. So she accepted and named her own conditions: That he give her two copies of the deeds of the house so that she could make her own investigation to see that everything was in order.

- Everything is in order- The man said.

- Yes, I know- Said my mother- but if you would be so kind as to lend me those copies I will be very grateful.

Finally he gave her the copies. My mother consulted a notary that was the husband of a friend of hers to make sure everything was in order. She was afraid that the property would be part of a common land, but no, it was private property and everything was in order.

The day of the appointment came. The notary's office was downtown, so it was much easier to take the subway. My mother gave me the pieces of jewelry to carry. She sewed them to a ribbon and put the ribbon around my neck like a necklace. Then she asked me to hide it under my shirt and put on a jacket so it wouldn't show.

- And be calm- She told me- Just imagine you're wearing one of those leather necklaces.

On the way I tried to think that and to act as normally as I could. I don't know if I succeeded, but when we finally arrived at the notary's office I felt relieved.

In a small meeting room, the owner of the house and his wife, the jewelry appraiser and another man who may or may not have been the notary were already waiting for us. He was probably one of the lawyers who worked at the Notary's office.

I went to the bathroom, took off my jacket, untangled myself from the jewelry, and gave it to my mother.

My brother was waiting for us in the meeting room. As soon as my mother and I returned to it, the man asked. Where is the jewelry?

My mother took it out and put it on a black cloth that was extended on the appraiser's table. He looked it over with a magnifying glass that he placed in one of his eyes. He examined it meticulously, first the rings, there where two of them, and then the watch. I was nervous about the verdict.

- Yes - he said – It is very good jewelry.

The man smiled, his wife didn't. My mother had instructed my brother and me very well not to show any emotion, so we were very serious, but on the inside I was relieved and I wanted to shout and jump for joy.

They signed the contract and my mother handed over a check that covered 50% of the price as an advance. On the day of the signing she would cover the other 50% and she would hand over the jewelry. As for the man, he would deliver the house.

I went back to the bathroom, hid the jewelry again, and we went home. I was so happy, I couldn't believe that we were going to have our own house. We would have our own place to go, no one would ask for it back. It was great!

A few days later the phone rang. My mother answered the phone. I couldn't hear what she said but as I passed next to her I saw how she suddenly grew pale and said angrily:

- Look, you and I signed a contract and I'm not going to allow you to go back on it. So I'll see you in two weeks for the signing.
- What happened?- I asked.

My mother sat on a chair in the dining room and tried to catch her breath. She was so upset she couldn't get the words out. My brother heard and came in.

- Are you all right? What happened? He asked her.
- I think everything is all right. The man from the house called and said someone else made a better offer on the house and that he was going to take it and not sell it to me, but I told him he couldn't go back on our agreement because we signed a contract and I already gave him an advance on the house. I hope he is convinced... she sighed.

I hoped everything would be all right. I was very tired. Besides, we had to pack everything for the move to the new house. I went up to my room to put my things in boxes. It was better not to think too much about it.

Thank God, the man didn't call again. The day of the signing of the contract before the notary he soberly signed the deeds, handed over the house keys, took the check and the jewelry and left with a simple "See you later".

We, on the other hand, hugged each other and leapt for joy.

God always manifests himself, and sometimes in the most unexpected ways. Even now, telling the story of how that peasant insisted that my brother go see that house, I am moved to tears. Thank God. For us it was a great blessing.

That same week we had to move and deliver the other house. So we went to clean the Homun house[14], our house. As I already described, it was a very simple house with strange proportions. The first thing we did was paint the front white and ask Mr. Margarito to help us transplant the pine trees to the right so we could park the cars. We moved. It was a wonderful feeling, knowing you were coming home.

My mother bought the sink that was missing from the bathroom and we removed the tapestries with different designs that covered the walls of what would be our rooms. That summer we worked on fixing the house up like mad. Two rooms were at the end of the inside of the house and there were another two small rooms on the left side of the house in the back of the garage, totally separated from the rest of

---

[14] The street name was Homun

the house. There was no direct access to them from inside the house. You had to go out to the garden, cross the parking space, and go up a few steps in order to go in. My brother took that room. Little by little, we fixed up the house. Unfortunately, there were some inconveniences. We didn't have a phone and the only public phone available in the area was about fifteen minutes away by foot. Since many people in that neighborhood didn't have a phone either, you always had to wait in a long line in order to make your call. The other inconvenience was that water didn't come very often so you had to shower fast so you wouldn't run out of water when you were in the middle of your shower, all soapy. That happened to me. And the third inconvenience was that, in those days, it was a bit far away, and not just anyone wanted to go there.

All of this took second stage when I thought that is was our house, nobody was going to raise the rent or ask us to vacate it, and that was fantastic.

Chapter 9

My father's job in Tijuana didn't last long, so he was back home. I don't remember how long he was there for this time, but it wasn't much.

December holidays were coming up, and on this occasion we were not going to Xalapa, we were staying home. Christmas dinner was a very simple affair. There were no guests, just the four of us. I went to sleep with my mother because now my father slept in what was somehow my room. I wouldn't know exactly what time in the morning it was, but something woke me up and as I turned my head and opened my eyes I felt a weapon pointed at my head and I screamed:

- Ohhhh!
- Shut up! - Said the hooded man that had the weapon on my head.

Obviously, I shut up.

- What's going on? - My mother woke up.
- Shut up, bitch! - The man answered her.

My mother and I sat on the bed without saying a word. Stubby, our black Cocker Spaniel, started to bark incessantly.

- Shut him up, make him shut up! - Said the man.

Try as I might to make him be quiet, I couldn't do it. A few minutes later my father appeared, his hands and feet tied with a blanket. He could barely walk. He looked at us and without saying anything he sat next to us on the bed.

We knew nothing of my brother. His room was outside. Maybe he didn't even know what was going on inside the house. What if something had happened to him? We had no clue. The curtains of the room were closed, you couldn't look out to the garden. Fortunately, a few minutes later they brought him in and forced him to sit next to us.

- Where's the safe? They asked.
- There's no safe. My mother answered.
- Don't try to fool us bitch! And tell me where it is!
- Honestly, I swear there is no safe.

The man left. We didn't move from the room.

- Give me the car keys!
- They're in the kitchen. My mother answered.
- Well give them to me!

My mother stood up. I think she went to the kitchen to give the man the keys to our white Atlantic. She came back and a little while later there was a great silence. We didn't move. We didn't talk. There were no voices to be heard. Minutes later I asked:

- Are they gone?
- I don't know. My brother said.
- Better not move and wait a little longer. My mother answered.

My father had gone mute. Facing the impotence of the situation he had nothing to say. We stayed that way, I don't know how long, until finally we dared to get up and leave the room. There was no one.

They had, of course, taken the car, the TV's, the toaster, the VCR, the few gold earrings and bracelets I had (they had been gifts from when I had turned fifteen) but, most importantly, they had taken away our peace of mind.

It was the morning of December 25th, 1987.

We notified the District Attorney Office of the robbery and the next day a team of investigators came to the house and asked us questions and took samples of fingerprints and photographed the house. They never found the culprits. What they did find was the car, completely ruined. It was a total loss.

A few weeks later I found out that my grandparents, my mother's parents, had lost their whole patrimony. Bad decisions had been taken and with the stock market crash on October, 1987, they had lost everything. Their house, their coffee farms, everything. My mother went to Xalapa for a few days. School was starting and my brother and I couldn't miss classes. Those were the first days of January 1988. We were afraid. So my brother stayed the night at one of his friend's houses and I stayed with my friend Estela. On January 5th I agreed to meet ′my brother at the house in Homun to get some things we needed. We were in for a surprise. The house had been robbed again. This time there wasn't much left to rob. The others had taken care of that. What was left was a black and white TV that was in the kitchen and a small oven that worked more as a toaster.

The window in the living room was open. We were so scared that in thirty seconds we took what we needed and got in the car to go to the public telephone in order to notify my mother.

- Are you all right?
- Yes- We answered- There was no one there when we got there.
- Oh well - She said when we told her what had happened.
- Try to be calm. I'll be back tomorrow.

That night at my friend's house, I was anything but calm. I couldn't fall asleep. On the one hand, I felt safe to be sleeping in her apartment in Villa Olimpica, but I was nervous about the robbery. Finally I went to sleep. The odd thing was that in the middle of my dreams I saw a very white light and I heard my mother's voice saying: "Be calm, my daughter".

I slept soundly, but I didn't forget that strange occurrence from my dream. The next day when we saw my mother I asked her:

- Mami, by any chance did you think about me very much last night?
- Yes- She said - I could hear you were very nervous over the phone and I was very worried about you, so worried that I

said out loud: "Be calm, my daughter". I wanted to hold you and comfort you.

I didn't want to go back to that house. I was very scared. But we didn't have many choices. We could only go to the tiny apartment that my grandparents were renting. We spoke to the landlady and she gave us permission to stay there for only one month. On entering the apartment you immediately stumbled upon the dining room that was to the right of a small kitchen. You crossed the dining room (in four steps) and there was a small living room, the bathroom and a bedroom at the end. The three of us could sleep in the living room. My mother on the couch and my brother and I would take turns sleeping on the floor in a sleeping bag and on a kind of couch made up of an individual chair and a center table.

It wasn't bad, I thought.

At least here we were safe. The bad news was that we could only stay there for a month. After that, we had to go back.

I don't know how my mother managed to get the money to block the garage door so that people could no longer look in, and to put glass on the whole fence that surrounded the house.

Also, we thought it would be a good idea to get a big dog that would stay in the garden in order to scare people away. "If they had to choose between robbing a house without a dog or one with a dog, they'd probably choose the one without it". Now I understood why almost all the neighbors had one or two dogs in their yards.

"There is no deadline that doesn't arrive and no date that doesn't come around". We returned to the house on Homun.

Someone gave us two small Weymaraners. And shortly after a friend called and asked if I would like an Alaska Malamute. Why not? We accepted.

The house was like a zoo. There was Stubby, the Cocker Spaniel and my cat inside the house, and outside there were the (at that moment) small Weymaraners and the Alaska Malamute. One of the Weymaraners got sick with distemper and died. So we were left with Kafka (the Weymaraner) and Poirot (the Alaska Malamute) taking care of the house. Thank God, no one ever robbed us again.

Chapter 10

I was about to finish junior high school. I wanted to go to high school in a different school. I was a little tired of the environment in the school I was in and especially of the teachers. Some of them still had that kind of medieval mentality in which they thought that the more students failed their class, the better teachers they were.

- Mami, I would like to transfer to the Inhumyc.
- All right- My mother answered- Only you'll have to do all the paperwork yourself and manage to keep your scholarship. I'm very busy at work and the truth is I hadn't considered the expense of your tuition. At the Green Hills School your scholarship is assured. But of course you can do it.

She didn't have to tell me twice. I immediately went to the Inhumyc to ask for information on the process of admission.

- You have to fill out this form, pay for the entrance exam, bring your grades and a letter of good conduct. The secretary told me.

I did what she told me as soon as possible. Everything was ready. I just had to pass the entrance exam and then, of course, I would worry about the scholarship, but one thing at a time.

- Look, it's nothing to worry about, but this high school is in great demand. Around 400 people apply and we only accept 80. The secretary told me as she stamped my papers.

Well, at least there was nothing to worry about! I don't know what I would have been able to say, had I wanted to.

The day of the exam came. And yes, there was a turmoil of people wanting to get into the Inhumyc. I looked for the classroom that had been assigned to me, I took out my pencil, eraser, everything that was necessary, and I waited for the person who was going to give us the test. The exam consisted of four parts and we had a limited amount of time to answer it. Finally, at around seven that evening, the process was completed. In one week you had to go see the secretary in the admissions office, the same one who had not been encouraging, to pick up the results.

The week felt like an eternity. The day I went to pick up the results I was afraid to cross the office doors and look at the secretary's face and for her to say "Oh well, I told you we only admit 80". No. I didn't have to think that, on the contrary, I had to think that I would see her and she would say: "Congratulations! You have been accepted!" I have always battled with my mind. I always go for the fatalistic news. The fact is that I crossed that door towards the unknown and there she was. The dreaded secretary that was to bear of the news.

- Hello, I'm here for the results of the test. Did I pass?
- I don't know. What's your name? - She asked shortly.
- Patricia Piña.
- Let me see - She left in search of the box full of envelopes. The fingers of her hands did not pass one by one. Finally she stopped on one. She verified my name and handed it to me.
- Here you are.

Gulp. My mouth was dry and my hands were shaking. I had thought of making it exciting like in those movies where the envelope remains unopened on the dining table until the family gathers around it and they all look at the results together. What was I thinking! This is real life. Please! It's four o'clock in the afternoon and your family gathers together at eleven at night. I opened the envelope. My eyes searched rapidly for the news that my mind wanted to register, but I was reading so fast I couldn't understand anything. So I took a deep breath. I sat down on the cement bench outside the school and I read calmly.

I had been accepted! I had done it! Thank you. Thank you. I was very happy. Quickly I went to find a working pay phone in order to call my mother and give her the news.

- Ministry of Interior -A voice answered.
- May I speak with Bertha Piñero?
- Who's calling?
- Her daughter.
- Oh yes. One moment please.

A few seconds later, my mother answered the phone.

- Hello.
- Mami. I passed. I picked up the results and I passed the Inhumyc entrance exam.
- What good news! Congratulations!

I still had to take care of the next part. I had to transfer my scholarship. At the Green Hills School I had a 100% scholarship and it was important that I keep it.

So I decided at that moment to return to the admissions office to ask about the requirements in order to request the scholarship.

The news was not good. The school only gave two scholarships per grade in high school. The truth is I don't know how much paperwork my mother did but she managed to get the second scholarship for me. I was ready to enter the Inhumyc.

The first day of classes was exciting. I was looking forward to entering high school and meeting new people. A different school. I was a little tired from having gone to the same school for fifteen years.

The Inhumyc was huge and so was my generation. In the first year of high school there were six classrooms with forty people in each of them. Two hundred and forty students! As I entered my classroom the feeling of not knowing anyone was odd. I had been assigned to classroom B and my friend Estela had also transferred schools to the Inhumyc and she had been assigned the classroom D. The good news was that most of us were in the same situation except for a small group who had finished junior high at the Inhumyc so we were all eager and open to making new friends.

Chapter 11

My great friend in high school was Roberta. We were both in the same group for the three years of high school so we shared our lives, our dreams, and our plans throughout those times.

During the second year of high school my family situation grew more complicated and Roberta and her family were my salvation.

My brother had entered University and his class schedules were terrible because he had class at seven in the morning, then another class at two in the afternoon, the next one was at four, and the last one was at eight in the evening. It was impossible for him to come home for dinner.

My mother, as I already mentioned, worked all day, so it was impossible for her to come home for dinner as well, and my father lived in Xalapa. So I had to eat alone every day. When I got home from school I went into the kitchen thinking about what I would make myself to eat. My options were: Roast beef with lettuce salad or roast beef with lettuce salad. "I know! I'll have roast beef with lettuce salad!" In the kitchen there was a small round table with three chairs. In front of the table there was a piece of furniture that had a TV on top that kept me company while I ate. Actually I didn't really watch anything, I just liked the noise it made because it made me feel less lonely. After that, I would get uncontrollably sleepy and I would take a nap, maybe for an hour. When I woke up I would do my homework, listen to music, go out to the garden for a while, watch TV again and there would come a moment when I wouldn't know what else to do. It was only eight o'clock. It was dark and no one would be home until about ten. What to do? I read a while, listened to music again, danced, and turned on the TV again. It's nine o'clock, I told myself. It was time to start preparing supper. For supper there were more options. *Quesadillas*, cereal, spaghetti, salad. The menu changed as the days went by.

Nine thirty. I had just taken the first bite of my quesadilla when I heard the honking of the car horn in the distance.

Good! It was by brother! As quickly as I could I took the keys to open the living room door and then the door to the garden in order to open the gate for him so he could pull the car into the garage. I was so happy to see him!

- Hello Isha. How are you? -He would ask
- Very well. How are you? How was school?
- Good -And he would tell me about his day.

I was so happy he was home!

- Do you want some supper? I made myself some *quesadillas*. Would you like some?
- Sure, thanks- He would answer.

That conversation became a routine. When my brother arrived I would make supper for him. When we were almost done we would hear the honking of my mother's car. It was necessary for us to open the gate for her as soon as we could because if it took us a little longer my mother would get worried and say:

- What happened? Why didn't anyone answer?
- Mami, that's what we were doing.
- Well, you took long and I was getting worried.
- Mami don't worry, we are on our way.

Obviously there were no cell phones, so we didn't know how to let her know that we were safe at home and that for whatever reason it was going to take us a little longer to open the gate. It was then that it occurred to us to turn a light on and off as a signal that everything was ok and that we were on our way.

My mother would arrive and then we would keep her company while she ate.

Why was my friend Roberta my salvation? Because she would invite me to her house now and then for dinner, and to spend the afternoon with her. My mother would pick me up on her way home from work. Sometimes those invitations would become more frequent. Once or twice a week. By the end of that year I would stay over for dinner almost every day.

Her mother, Mrs. Paz, always welcomed me with open arms and I slowly won over Gladys, their maid. At first she would scold Roberta that she had to give notice before inviting people over because the orange juice she made was just enough for the people she was expecting. Towards the end of those years, Gladys would scold me when I didn't eat dinner there and Roberta didn't let her know because there had been orange juice left over from what she had made, thinking that I would eat there.

When the invitations became more frequent, at first I was embarrassed. Roberta would say:

- Isha, come to dinner to my house.
- No, I can't today.
- Why? What are you doing?
- Nothing - I thought to myself and kept quiet.
- See. You don't have to do anything special. Come to my house. What are you going to do all alone at your house? Call your mom and ask her for permission.

She would convince me immediately. So we would go to the phone that was at the entrance of the school and I would call my mom and ask for her permission. I think she thought the same thing Roberta said. It was better for me to be at my friend's house than alone at my house. Even though it meant she would have to make a 20-minute detour on her way home because Roberta's house wasn't exactly on the way.

Chapter 12

Roberta and I talked about everything, we talked about our plans when we would finish high school. My plans were to finish high school, go to work at some transnational company, maybe live alone for a while and then get married and have children.

My friend Roberta had other plans. She wanted to get married immediately! Have kids, preferably a girl and a boy. She had already decided that when they would be three or four she would dress them alike so even their shoelaces matched. She was really into graphic design, so she had no doubts about what she wanted to study, of course, being married and while the kids came.

I, on the contrary, was very confused as to what I wanted to study. I was only sure of two things. On one hand, I knew I didn't want to study medicine and on the other, I knew I didn't want to study Law. Other than that, so many options went through my head. The first was Psychology. It was logical that I was influenced by my Psychology teacher, the psychologist Gabriel Ortiz, a great person who had helped me through the tumultuous years of my adolescence. But I wasn't sure it was really my path, sometimes I though that I had enough personal problems to solve without solving other people's. Besides, the first restriction came up when I found out that in order to study Psychology you had to have studied Area 2 (Chemistry-Biology), and I had studied area 3 (Economics-Administration). I had taken this decision based on a comprehensive analysis of subjects that I no longer desired to take. In my decision making process I had used this grandiose methodology, a completely erroneous one. In area 1 (physics-mathematics) you had the disadvantage, of having to study physics, which was not precisely my strong subject. Area 2 had the disadvantage of having to study biology, biology lab and anatomy, which was torture for me because of my terrible memory. It had been almost impossible during fifth grade for me to learn the bones of the face of the human body, let alone the muscles. On top of everything else, you had to stay at school during Friday afternoons in order to finish the lab assignments. Area 4 presented the problem of Law, of which I had had enough. Given my theory of restrictions I had decided on Area 3 (economic-administration), and unfortunately while practicing this silly process, the first consequence had presented itself: I couldn't even be considered for the admissions exam to Psychology.

My second option was Graphic Design. Of course! I was being influenced again, but it happens to everyone. My friend liked it so much, why shouldn't I like it? Some years ago I had enjoyed oil painting and sometimes watercolors... so I thought Graphic Design was made for me.

That is how Roberta and I went to ask about the requirements at the Intercontinental University (UIC in Spanish) for presenting the admissions exam. There were several of them. There was a basic knowledge test, a practical drawing test, an interview with the Director of the faculty in which you had to explain the reasons why you wanted to study Graphic Design, and lastly, you had to go through several medical tests so that they knew you were healthy.

Well, I thought, it's not so complicated. Besides, my brother had told me that anyone who wanted to get into the UIC could, unless you really didn't have the capability.

Roberta and I went to the University, feeling very grown up, to pick up the applications that we had to fill in. Very kindly the lady at the desk asked us:

- Would you like the guide?
- Yes, of course. We answered.
- There's an extra cost.

Neither of us were economically prepared for that, so that extra cost changed our minds.

- Well, don't worry. We'll be fine without the guide.

We paid for our test, and a doubt came over me about whether it would have been better to buy the guide and I told Roberta: - Hey, why do you think she insisted on our buying the guide? Do you think there is a lot of material? For me back then and even today, when someone asks me something in that way, I feel an insistence that should be taken into account since in Mexico so many things are said "under the table" or insinuated so one must learn to read between the lines. But at that moment I was still learning the concept. I tried to calm myself by telling myself that the guide was not that important, that I was a good student, I had one of the best grade averages in my high school and surely it would just be a test of general knowledge. Besides, at home the economic situation was difficult and that way I wouldn't have to ask my mother for more money to buy the guide. The expense of the admission exam had already been enough, an extra expense on our already tight budget. At that moment I couldn't afford to ask for more.

Ahhhhh! I felt a great load of my mind as I convinced myself.

We were ready for the challenge that lay ahead of us.

The day of the written exam came. Of course, as is natural at nineteen, Roberta and I arrived together. Unfortunately for us, the seating arrangements for the exams were in alphabetical order according to your last name so Garcia was to go to one classroom and Piña to another.

Good luck Roberta, and remember not to leave any questions in blank, even if you have to make up the answer. You might get it right anyway.

This piece of advice had been given to us by a teacher who told us never to leave any questions unanswered in a test.

Thanks and good luck to you too - Answered Roberta.

We went into the classroom, sat down at the desks, and the exams were handed out to us. I couldn't believe it, the exam was at least 30 pages long. I started to get a little nervous, or a lot nervous, because as I read the questions of the exam I realized how few answers I knew and it was more and more frequent that I had to use my teacher's advice. Guess what? The test was multiple choice, so maybe it was a, b, c, or d. Finally, I finished. I didn't have the nerve, or the capacity, or the will to double-check my answers so I just handed it in. As I left, I realized the importance of that guide and I understood the lady's insistence.

Roberta did just as badly as me, we felt a little low but well, it was just one part of the long admissions process. We still had possibilities, because if we proved our capacity for drawing and our enthusiasm for studying Graphic Design at the UIC, well, the admissions exam couldn't be that important. The next day we had to present the practical exam. We had to make different figures in technical drawing. I was secretly trying to remember the lessons in technical drawing that I had taken in junior high school, because in area 3 there were no lessons in technical drawing, so the idea was a bit fuzzy for me. I did what I could but the hexagon didn't exactly come out with all the sides in the same size. Then you had to copy an apple. I copied it. End of the exam. Things had not gone so bad. We had a sandwich and a soda while the time came for the interviews.

My interview was at six that evening, so while the time came my anxiety grew. What were they going to ask me? Why I wanted to study Graphic Design? I couldn't very well answer that my friend was very sure that that was what she wanted to study and that I really didn't have the slightest idea but that I thought that it could be… fun? "What are you thinking Patricia! You can't answer that, in that very moment your few possibilities will vanish!" What to say, what to say. Six o'clock came, six thirty, seven, seven thirty. What was going on?! Finally they called my name –Patricia Piña, please present yourself at the Coordinator's office.

It was nighttime, I was tired. The classroom where the interview was to be held was lighted with white light and white light has always had an intimidating effect on me. And at that time at night, after all the interviews he had already conducted, the coordinator was tired and in a bad mood. I had a feeling that this wasn't going to be the best interview of my life.

- Hello. He said. He lowered his gaze to look for my name.
- Let's see, Patricia, and why do you want to study Graphic Design?

Oh, no! There was the dreaded question.

– Well, I said, trying to make my voice sound confident

- I want to study Graphic Design because I think it is a very important career… Ha, ha, even I wasn't buying this idea, at that moment I was a bit confused about what was important in my life. And I continued in a confident, paused voice…

- Because we can capture and transmit all of our sensitivity towards the outer world. Besides, at this moment in time the way that companies present their products is more important than ever. Magnificent, I thought, that was very good. The coordinator simply looked down, jotted something down and thanked me, signaling the way out with his arm.

Whaaaaaat! I had waited almost three hours for that?! I couldn't believe it. I felt an anger and frustration that demanded a cigarette. I lit my cigarette, furious, as Roberta appeared.

- How did it go? I asked her.
- Really well. She answered. The coordinator is a very nice lady and we talked for about twenty minutes.
- What? Lady? I was interviewed by a man for about twenty seconds.
- And how did it go? Roberta asked.
- You can imagine. I told her. If the interview lasted twenty seconds. In the end, I said (more for my own comfort than for hers), if they don't take me it will be a sign that Graphic Design is not for me.

The next day we would be given our medical examinations, which consisted of a blood test and some X-rays of our spines. The results were that I was a bit anemic and my spinal cord looked like a serpent. Surely the exams had not been done properly. How could that be, when I hadn't ever had any back pains or anything! The anemia problem had a solution, but the back situation could be a problem since if I wanted to study Graphic Design. I would have to spend long hours in front of a drawing board and surely that wouldn't be good for me.

The next week we had to go to the University to get the results. The list was glued to the windows of the classrooms in the Graphic Design area. As I got closer to the windows I felt how my heart started to pound faster and faster. On one hand, I thought it was not possible that I wouldn't be accepted. I had an excellent high school grade average and I thought of myself as a "smart" girl, but on the other hand, I knew I hadn't done well on the tests and, smart as I might feel, I had not bought and studied the guide and the practical exam had been a disaster, not to mention the interview.

On the list, only the names of the people who had been accepted appeared, alphabetically by last name. Check the list as I might, my last name was not on it. I checked again and again in the hope that I hadn't read correctly, perhaps my eyes had skipped my last name… but no, it wasn't there, I had not been accepted. My friend Roberta hadn't been accepted either, and for a moment I felt relieved. She was so sure of her calling, mixing colors all day, and she hadn't met the profile. Now that I remember those times, I think of how stupid and arrogant I was.

I said goodbye to my friend Roberta, we were both feeling kind of low. How was it possible that we had not been accepted? Had we not been born to be graphic designers? Such is life. In my case, I knew that I had to think of some other career.

Chapter 13

My mother worked all day at the Ministry of Interior. Her schedule, like most people's work schedules in Mexico, made it difficult to be close to me at the time. She worked from 10:30 in the morning to 10:30 at night. But she had a three hour lunch hour. Think about it. Three hours! That should be enough for a person to go home, have lunch, and come back, but unfortunately in Mexico City that is practically impossible, especially since most people live about an hour and a half in traffic away from their workplaces. So it was impossible for my mother to go from Bucareli to the Ajusco for lunch. At the end of the day she would arrive exhausted at eleven to chat with her children like a zombie about her day.

Ever since then and up until now I ask myself: Why are schedules in Mexico like that? In other parts of the world schedules are from eight in the morning to five in the afternoon, in this way the family has the rest of the day to coexist, talk, and rest, but that was not my reality. In Mexico things weren't like that and they still aren't like that, so when a mom needs or wants to work, she is torn between the choice of working or tending to her family. On many occasions they need to juggle many things at once in order to more or less satisfy the different worlds that they occupy with a level of stress that is hard to describe, trying to care for their children, trying to make their husbands understand and trying to meet their obligations at work. Why isn't there a reasonable work schedule in Mexico?

I took the bus that passed in front of the UIC in order to get to my house. The bus ran a route that was called "Carretera" and went all the way through the Hidalgo neighborhood until it got to the Picacho-Ajusco freeway. I would get off at Homun street and had to go around the block given the city´s insecurity and especially that neighborhood's. The neighbors had agreed to close down certain streets with some big pots that obligated you to enter through a guardhouse (in which there was no guard), but anyway this measure made the neighbors feel safer somehow. For me it meant an extra twenty minute walk to my house after a forty five minute bus ride that for some reason did not make any stops except those which the passengers demanded when they wanted to get on or off. So sometimes in a scope of 150 meters the bus would stop five times, and that would make the ride even longer.

During the ride endless thoughts went through my head and none in special. My mind was wandering. I blamed myself from not having bought the guide to not making the right decision. Why wasn't I one of those people who know from the beginning what they wanted to do with their lives? I didn't have the foggiest idea. It was March. Most of my schoolmates were clear on their paths. Some of them would take a six-month break and would travel around the world, others were already accepted in Universities and would continue with their careers. What about me? What was I going to be? How was I going to tell my mother that I hadn't passed the entrance exam? How was I going to tell my brother, whom back then had such authority over me that I had failed the entrance exam to a university where even the stupidest person could pass? I tried to justify myself to myself that he really just said those things in order to brag a little because he studied actuary at the ITAM[15], of course to him everything seemed simple to him, but to me it wasn't. It had been a hard test and I had failed it.

Finally we arrived at the corner where I had to get out, and in the midst of pushes and shoves I asked a young man to please push the button that was on top of the back door that indicated that someone needed to get out.. Sometimes the bus was so full that you had to yell "Getting out!" so the bus wouldn't take off while you were still getting out and drag half your book bag along with it. I was able to get out. I walked the five remaining blocks at a slow but alert pace. In those areas you had to be aware of the people who passed you by. I had probably become a bit paranoid after the assault to our house in the early hours of a beautiful Christmas morning, but it was worth it to take precautions.

At home there were five dogs. Two of them were in the garden, another two on the roof of the house, and one lived inside the house. So every time you got near the house a

---

[15] A very prestigious university in Mexico and the world

concert of barking would start that showed the dog's joy at someone coming home. I always pulled my keys out a block before getting home. I liked to be prepared to open the door as quickly as possible out of fear that someone would surprise me while I was opening the door to the house. I got home. As always, only the dogs were there to welcome me, my mother and my brother would get home late at night. I can't remember if I burst into tears, but I probably did, I have a great talent for crying, I feel that it is easier to digest difficulties that way, although I really think that it is a sign of immaturity.

At night first my brother and then my mother arrived and asked how I had done, and when I told them I hadn't passed the test, they both went mute, then said - "Oh well, sometimes that happens", and that there would be another chance. I secretly thought that in that University there would definitely not be another chance.

Chapter 14

The days passed by and as the end of the school year came closer my indecision increased. I had thought about studying Tourism, it was a career that had subjects I liked, besides cooking, traveling, and staying in hotels. I changed my mind though, when my mother told me that it was a great idea to study Tourism, except when the time came for me to do my social service in hotels, I wouldn't have permission. I guess it was dumb of me, but at the time that had a big impact on me, and I cancelled that option.

One day at the Inhumyc I was called because someone from the Tecnologico de Monterrey wanted to talk to us. Us? Who? In the central courtyard we gathered, about ten people. The person from the TEC was a kind woman that invited us to a breakfast at the University facilities at Mexico City in order for us to get to know it and see the different careers they offered. The TEC (as it is known in Mexico) was just opening then. It had huge grounds at the south of the city and was painted hot pink. On the ground floor was the cafeteria (if you could call it that). On the second floor were the administrative offices and the professors´ cubicles, and all the other floors were classrooms.

The invitation was to breakfast that Saturday in the morning, and as always I was there at 9:30 on the nose. No one had arrived. In Mexico we have the odd custom of always making appointments half an hour earlier than we actually expect them to happen, and I have the bad habit of always arriving on time, but it is a habit I have never been able to shake off.

Little by little the rest of the guests arrived, high school students from different schools in Mexico City. We were served a delicious breakfast and afterwards we were led to an exhibit with different stands, each one representing one of the careers that were offered at the University. To my surprise I ran into a stand that represented the Marketing career. What was that? I had never heard of marketing, it was 1991. Maybe in other environments it was more well known, but not to me. At that stand there were Kellogg's packages, Procter and Gamble leaflets, Colgate products. Interesting. I went up to the stand to ask about the career curriculum and they told me about some of the subjects that you studied and I got an idea of what you could work in. A little sales, a little... surveying? Publicity, consumer satisfaction... it looked very interesting. I took a brochure and sat down to read it calmly. There were subjects that I liked a lot like publicity, market research, graphic design, and I had no idea about other subjects, but anyway it seemed a much more broad view than graphic design. Besides, the ITESM had given me some great news. All of us who had been invited to the breakfast were the best grade averages in our schools and therefore had many possibilities of obtaining a scholarship. Magnificent! I needed a scholarship. I had had one since the first year of junior high school and I knew that at home there was not enough money to pay for a private Collage tuition. If the TEC gave me this benefit it could be a great opportunity for me.

That same day I requested the information I needed in order to present the admissions exam and to request the scholarship. They gave me the brochures. You had to fill in a form, pay for the admissions exam and without an extra charge they gave you a small study guide. It was not going to happen to me again, I had to pass that exam. So I started studying the guide. It was not exactly what I had imagined. I had expected a guide where you had to memorize certain information that would surely be asked during the test. But no, this was different. There was a section where you had to select a figure that would best complete a puzzle. There was a math part where there were different kinds of problems and exercises that you had to solve, and the third part was Spanish. In the guide there was a text that you had to read and understand so later you could answer questions about it. I couldn't believe it. Surely I had not understood something or they had given me an abridged version of the study guide, a version that had no extra cost. There must be a longer study guide like the one at the UIC. So the next day I called the TEC in order to ask about the real study guide and how I could get it. To my surprise there was no "real" study guide, the only guide was the one they had given me when I paid for my admission exam, so that was it.

I think I must have gone over the four pages of the guide at least ten times. I did what I had always done when I had a difficult test, I reviewed and reviewed and reviewed in order not to forget anything.

The day of the exam came. All the aspiring students were sat in an auditorium, a very nice one; in the front was the forum and there was a rectangular table covered with a navy blue mantel on top of which the examinations were piled and next to them, a bunch of pencils. We sat in the stands where, to my surprise, on one side, where you rested your arm, a small writing table slid out.

The moment had arrived, we were all sitting down and they passed out the tests and the pencils. My hands were sweating, I felt my face burning, I tried to breathe deeply in order to calm my nerves and concentrate on the exam. I answered the best I could, of course there were questions I wasn't sure of, but I answered them anyway. I finished and double-checked my test once more as the bell that announced that time was up rang. I was done. Three days later we had to go to the Office of Student Affairs to pick up the results.

Three days later I was there standing in line. I don't know if I felt more nervous at that moment or at the moment of answering the test. The wait seemed eternal, I doubted I had passed and my mind shot ahead to when I would be lamenting myself and wondering what I would do if I was rejected again. At that moment two boys interrupted my thoughts, they were waiting in line as well. They seemed familiar but I couldn't remember where I had seen them before. My memory has always been a bit slow but finally I remembered them, I had talked to one of them during the breakfast, but I didn't know where I knew the other one from, and the most surprising thing was that they looked so much alike that I didn't know if the one I had talked to during the breakfast was the one with blue eyes or the one with brown ones, so in order to avoid mistakes I greeted them both at the same time. Hello! How are you? Are you here for your results too? – Yes. The one with blue eyes answered. I don't know how I did.

Since the beginning they had told us that the number that was written on our admission token would be our enrollment number and that we should guard it with our lives. We had to memorize it because it was the only way they would give us the information about our tests and that if we were accepted that number would be everything to us.

Gulp! What was my number? 7024… what? I had forgotten it and I didn't have the paper that they had given me when I paid for my admission exam. I couldn't go home and come back again, by that time the offices would be closed. I was nervous, besides not knowing whether I had passed or not, well, I wasn't going to know because I had forgotten the number of my life. To my comfort I heard:

- Pablo Wydler?

The boy with the brown eyes approached the window and was given an envelope. Suddenly he started jumping for joy. I inferred that he had been admitted.

- Carlos Wydler? The lady called.

Oh! They're brothers. I said to myself. That's why they look so much alike. And I tried to memorize their names in my head. Brown eyes, Pablo. Blue eyes, Carlos. Brown eyes, Pablo. Blue eyes, Carlos... I was very concentrated memorizing names when in the back of my mind, I heard:

- Patricia Piña.
- Hey, they're calling you. Who was it? Pablo? Carlos?
- Patricia Piña. The lady at the window called once more.
- It's me. I said.

As I walked over my heart was doing summersaults, my hands were shaking and my face was burning. I was given my envelope. I opened it immediately and I couldn't believe it! I had been accepted! Yupeeeee! I was going to the TEC! I had been accepted! So, I wasn't so dumb after all. They had recognized some virtue in me. I was accepted!

Now came the next part. I needed a scholarship. My parents had separated, although they had never divorced, when I was 18. My father lived in Xalapa and my brother and I lived with my mother in Mexico City. The economic situation in my house was complicated. My mother worked at the Ministry of Interior with a salary that barely covered our essential expenses. My father sometimes sent money, but you never knew when or how much he was going to send, so the scholarship was very necessary.

I went to the scholarship office to get the necessary information, there were a considerable amount of papers that you had to hand in: Bank statements, ID, forms to fill out, etc. So I began collecting and handing in all the documents that they asked for, and after that, I had to wait for the response that would be given to me in a week. At some moments the anxiety became intense.

What would happen if they didn't give it to me? Then what?

To my great fortune I got the scholarship. It wasn't a complete scholarship, that is, it didn't cover the 100% of the cost of the tuition, but they had given me a scholarship-credit of 75%, that is, 50% was a scholarship and 25% was credit to be paid once I had finished my studies. The other 25% had to be paid monthly.

It wasn't bad… Not bad at all. To tell the truth, it was really good! This scholarship system, new back then, gave me the possibility of studying a career. Of course, I had to keep an 8.5 grade average, I could never fail a subject, I was entitled to 50% less absences than students that did not have scholarships, and I had to work for a number of hours every week with some teacher that they would assign to me in order to realize my scholar service.

It doesn't matter. I thought. It was the first time I felt a certain clarity in my path, and that made me very happy.

Chapter 15

Every day life in high school continued as always, but as the end of the school year came nearer, certain events needed to be organized: The graduation ceremony and the graduation trip. Both events made me a bit nervous, especially because of the expenses. Sometimes I felt that it was putting too much pressure on my mother if I told her that I wanted to go to the ceremony and on the class trip. I had to make a decision and the trip appealed to me more than the ceremony did. It lost it's appeal because they were going to give us our diplomas and then there would be a dinner or something. The truth is I didn't even pay attention to what our class representative told us, and those of us who weren't going could go get our papers later. What interested me was the class trip.

As always, there were a group of "intellectuals" that wanted the trip to be an experience that would allow us to increase our knowledge and be better prepared for entering University. There was another group, a big one, that just wanted to have fun, go to a beach, no culture, just fun.

Of course, the teachers backed up the cultural plan, and of course, most of the students backed up the fun plan. I supported either, as long as it gave me the opportunity to go on a trip and have a change of scenery. If it was culture that was good; if it was the beach and fun, great. Let's get out of the city!

They came to an arrangement. It was going to be a mixed generation trip. The first three days were going to be cultural and we were going to go to Oaxaca to Monte Alban and Mitla[16], the "Tule"[17], the historic center of Oaxaca, and the other two days were going to the beach. Since we were going to be nearby we would go to Puerto Escondido[18].

The plan was to meet very early in the morning at the school in order to take the bus that would take us to Oaxaca. We would be there for three days and then we would go, again by bus, to Puerto Escondido and from

---

[16] Archeological sites in the State of Oaxaca
[17] A legendary tree that is more than two thousand years old
[18] A beach in the state of Oaxaca

there we would come back to Mexico City by a charter plane.

It was done. I don't know how my mother got the money for my trip, but she did it. I paid. I was ready. The trip would take place a little before final examinations. I knew that I was exempt for all subjects except for Civics. I just didn't get that subject. With my terrible memory, it was hard for me to remember the hundreds of thousands of articles of the Constitution that I was supposed to know by heart. Of course I know I'm exaggerating but that is how it felt to me and the teacher would just ask: Article 26, article 123? Etc. etc. And more articles. How was I supposed to learn them! If she would at least give me some other reference. But no. Well, I would worry about that later.

I was going on the trip. I packed my suitcase. Not a very big one because I have never liked carrying too much. That's why I decided that it was not necessary to pack the pillow or the blanket that they had advised us to pack. Why would I need a pillow, it would just be bulky. Besides, I could always make myself a little pillow with my sweater when I got sleepy. That way I didn't have to carry more things around. And a blanket! My friend Estela was just exaggerating. She said we should take one because it was very cold. If you got cold you could just put a sweatshirt on and that would be enough, why carry more?

I was ready. Every one of us was on a list that indicated what bus you had to take, with the warning that we were to learn the number of the bus because it would be our bus for the whole trip. The people that would share your hotel room would travel on that bus and the meals were all organized and included.

We left Mexico City. The first hours were all about fun, singing, listening to music on the tape recorder that someone had brought. As the time went by the singing calmed down, the shouting stopped and everyone started to talk with the person they were sitting with. Sometimes you would get up and sit on the arm of the seat of whomever you particularly wanted to talk to. We stopped to eat at a highway restaurant that had everything ready for us. And the trip continued, night came and the cold came and I was sleepy. Only a small inconvenience presented itself. In my eagerness to travel light I had not packed a pillow or a blanket and, as was logical, those who had were using theirs and I was freezing and so sleepy. I couldn't make a pillow out of my sweater because then I would have to take it off and get colder so I leaned against the window -at least I got a window seat, I thought- in order to get some sleep, but I couldn't. My head bounced against the glass like a soccer ball and the glass was as cold as a refrigerator. At that moment I felt truly miserable, not to have followed my friend's advice that was now sleeping comfortably with her pillow and her blanket and here I was… Oh well. We arrived. It was late at night. We were told which our rooms were and we went to sleep. I couldn't believe it! I was finally in a warm bed and… a pillow! I slept like a log. I fell asleep the moment I lay down. The next morning I woke up late, my roommates were ready: Showered, hair combed, dressed, and I… I had to choose whether to shower or to have breakfast, because the bus was leaving in forty minutes for the pyramids.

Believe it or not, the decision was a hard one. I had to shower. I had spent the day before on a bus, with temperature changes and I didn't exactly smell of roses. More like a little "acid". I jumped in the shower, and I think I was the number 250 out of 250 students to shower. The water was freezing! Even though I waited to find out which of the handles was the one for hot water, I didn't manage to get even lukewarm water to come out. I would try the one on the right and wait, and then turn on the one on the left and nothing. The water was still cold. That was when I decided that I had to take a really quick shower even if it was just to clean the most important parts.

One, two, three. I said to myself.

I quickly got wet, raised my arms, scrubbed and rinsed. Between my legs, same procedure. Hair, well, it wasn't so dirty.

- Ohhhh I can't take it anymore! Ready! Out!

I got dressed as quickly as possible. I threw on some jeans, a t-shirt, sweatshirt, sneakers. Dressed. Ponytail. Hair done. Ready. I ran out to see if by any chance there was any breakfast left. How naïve, of course there was nothing, but I found some toast and a little bit of dry marmalade on a table. I took it. It was better than nothing.

We got on the buses that had been assigned to us and headed towards the pyramids in Monte Alban. The drive was short. The view was marvelous. In the middle of the (somewhat neglected) desert landscape were the pyramids. They were a beauty.

We had permission to wander around a bit so Roberta and I went down the stairs and contemplated the landscape. We admired the frets that were engraved on the walls of the pyramids, the different rooms and hallways that created a kind of maze. I began to imagine what life must have been like back then. How was society organized? What was a normal day like for a person my age?

Our next stop was lunch! How wonderful, I was so hungry because the calming effect of the toast was gone. The little inn wasn't prepared to receive so many people so it took them a while to serve the food. The problem was that in order to calm the hunger pangs they brought us baskets of bread and saucers with salsa and I was so hungry that by the time the food came my hunger had diminished drastically.

It was a very nice trip. We also went to Mitla, the Tule, the historic center of Oaxaca and to the market, famous for it's exotic gastronomy. You could find ice cream there of the most extravagant flavors. Rose petal, mole, tequila, among others, besides the normal ones, vanilla, chocolate, nut, etc. You could also eat spicy grasshoppers, escamoles, maguey worms, and I don't know how many kinds of insects.

As was to be expected, we wanted to try these things. My economy was limited so I had to choose between the grasshoppers or the mole ice cream. I chose the grasshoppers. I approached the stand at the market that sold them. The salesperson or *marchante* as we call them in Mexico egged me on:

- Come on *güerita*, try them, they're very good.
- Just imagine you're trying some *chicharrón* with lemon and chile. Besides, *chicharrón* isn't good for you and the grasshoppers are full of protein.

I couldn't believe what I was about to do. They say love is born through the eyes, so it was better not to look at them. I took a grasshopper from the palm of the hand of the *marchante*. I closed my eyes, put it in my mouth, and tried to chew and "enjoy" the taste. The first thing I felt was something crunchy and thin that broke with my chewing, but the moment I felt a kind of paw stick in my tooth, I couldn't take it anymore. I swallowed without tasting and ran to buy a soda. I definitely preferred *chicharrón*, even if it wasn't good for me.

I belong to the kind of Mexican people who like to eat things we know. Roasted beef, chicken breasts, rice, beans, *tortillas*. I have never been very good at strange things like grasshoppers, escamoles, maguey worms, eye tacos, etc. They say Mexican, French, and Chinese cuisines are the three great cuisines of the world because they cook and eat everything, but not all of us do. I think I would have preferred the mole ice cream, at least there wouldn't have been anything strange in my mouth.

We left the City of Oaxaca behind us, the "cultural" part of the trip was over and we were headed to the "fun" part, Puerto Escondido. That journey was long, too. The cold of the sierra could be felt through the windows of the bus and through my lack of blanket. I managed to make myself a pillow out of a t-shirt that I didn't pack and rolled up, so at least I had a place to lean my head against so it didn't bounce against the window at every bump in the road that the bus passed on the highway.

We arrived. The hotel was very nice. Our room had a view of the sea. The sea at Puerto Escondido is a deep blue color, lapis lazuli, beautiful. Everyone's greatest concern was to enjoy and have fun. We spent the time on the beach, the pool, the gardens, getting tans and listening to music. On one occasion we had the choice of going to town or staying at the hotel. In those times I wasn't so enthusiastic so I decided to stay at the hotel, talking and having fun. When I realized that most people had gone to town it was too late to change my mind because the buses were gone.

Strangely, my friend Roberta had gone to town without me and when I least expected it Mauricio was sitting there. He had stayed too. Gulp! I started to feel nervous, a hole in my stomach, and I didn't know what to do.

Mauricio, Roberta, and I had been great friends during the first years of high school. On the third year we were in different classrooms. Roberta and I were in area 3, group A, and Mauricio was in group B. For some strange reason, after he found out that I liked him, the relationship became distant and for that school year we practically didn't speak to each other.

But that day he was sitting there on the edge of the fence looking towards the sea. His skin, tanned from the sun, contrasted with his green eyes beautifully. And here I stood, without daring to say or do anything. At that moment I realized I had to admit it, I still liked him. So I decided to lie in a beach chair close by and read. Ha ha ha. I didn't read a single line. I was nervous, my mind could not think about anything but him. I discreetly looked at him over the edge of my book and tried to see if there was any reaction from him. Nothing. He was still absorbed in his thoughts and I was absorbed in his movements. I had to concentrate on my book, that way those unending moments could end. Finally I did it, I read two sentences and I looked towards him again. Where had he gone? At that moment I heard:

- Hello Isha. You didn't go either?
- No… - I stuttered. I didn't.
- And, how are you? He asked.
- Well, fine, here, reading my book and resting - So many things were going through my head. What I could say that would be interesting so he would stay and talk to me. Nothing occurred to me,

my head was blank, what was wrong with me?

Little by little the conversation started to flow. Each of us asked ourselves what had happened.

-   I decided to go into area 3 because you guys had decided on area 3, but I was assigned a different group and I never heard from you again. Mauricio said.

I didn't expect that, however I felt that it was he who had drifted apart.

-   And also, especially because of you.

What! Because of me! I thought we were just friends although deep down, or maybe not even that deep down, I wanted him to like me. It was hard for me to accept what I was hearing.

-   I like you. I've always liked you. He said.

I was speechless. Three years of friendship and now he was admitting that he liked me. Just when we were finishing high school. I broke down, my heart was beating wildly, I felt myself growing red, green, blue, purple… and we kissed.

Later that night we had our farewell party, but Roberta didn't know that I was Mauricio's... girlfriend? And I didn't know how I was going to tell her about it. It was as if I had betrayed her because the three of us had always been friends, but now I asked myself if maybe she liked him too. She had never told me if she had any interest in him other than friendship, and I never asked her, but given the recent events I had to be honest with her. She was my best friend.

- What do you think happened while you were in town?
- What happened? Tell me! Roberta said.
- Well, I talked to Mauricio.
- Mauricio? He's been very strange this year, he has distanced himself, done his own thing.
- Well, yes, he told me something like that. And I quickly let out the news. He told me he's always liked me - Gulp. I had said it and she was quiet.
- But, how? Did you like Mauricio?

Ohhhhh, I didn't know what to say. How to tell her, yes, I had always liked him and I had never told her about it. So many years of friendship and I hadn't shared this feeling with her.

- Well, yes.
- Good! I'm happy for you. Come on, let's go to the party, it's starting.
- End of conversation. We never cleared up the subject.

The party was on the moonlit beach. We were all there, having a good time. It was the satisfaction of duty done and the dreams of new paths to travel. We had finished high school and each of us was going to construct our lives, take our paths.

Mauricio walked into the party and I started to shake. I don't know why I felt so nervous. It was such a strange feeling, because even though I had known him for years, that night it felt like I barely knew him. I didn't know how to act in front of him. Did I have to be with him all the time? What to talk about? My mind was blank. I simply didn't know what to say.

- Hello. You look pretty. He said.
- Hello. Thank you. I answered.
- Come on. Let's dance.

Sure. Let's dance. That way we don't have to talk. I thought.

We danced for the whole party. My friends looked at me filled with curiosity. I had only told Roberta that we were boyfriend and girlfriend, but I immediately realized that they all knew anyway. These kinds of news spread like wildfire.

The next day we went back to Mexico City. We took a charter flight. It was short, an hour. My mother and my brother were waiting for me in the arrivals gate at the airport. We went home.

The last two weeks of school were strange. Only the students that had to present the final exams would go and when we finished we could go home. So there weren't any formal classes and neither Mauricio nor I tried to find each other. I think that relationship was not working out as I had thought it would. I thought it would be different.

Chapter 16

One Friday Mauricio called me on the phone to my house to ask me to a gathering with his friends. When he went to pick me up I immediately felt a tension and distance between us.

- Hello. He greeted me.
- How are you?
- Good. I answered. What about you? How have you done with your exams?
- Good. Listen, the gathering is going to be at Rana´s house with my friends from my group.
- I know. You told me. The only thing is I only have permission until twelve.

Generally that's when the problems with my boyfriends started.

- What! Until twelve? That's very early. Besides, it's all the way in San Antonio.

Going all the way to San Antonio meant at least a half hour drive. That is, it was nine o'clock so we would arrive at nine thirty and we had only two hours to be at the gathering in order for me to be back home at twelve. That is how it was. My mother was not flexible when it came to night hours and I had to punctual if I knew what was good for me because even if I was ten or fifteen minutes late my mother would get angry. Now I understand her position better, it was logical that living in Mexico City she would worry about her daughter being out at night, also because my "boyfriend" would be driving me back. For her that situation must have been terrifying, but still she would give me permission. The whole responsibility of educating two teenagers fell upon her shoulders. She had to decide whether to give us permission or not. She would patiently listen to our account of things, good or bad, and she would unconditionally support us, advise us, and be there for us when we needed her, but it was evidently not an easy position to be in for her, because on top of everything else, she worked in order to support us. The money my father would send was not enough, and given his depression issues, it wasn't constant either.

The point is that that gathering was a disaster. I turned out to be too much of a good girl for his group of rock and roll friends. Mauricio simply didn't know what to do. He would talk to me and then talk to them. I would talk to him and then pretend to do something else, because I didn't talk to anyone else. It was one of those gatherings where you just feel completely out of place. I didn't know anyone. I was glad I had to get home early.

Mauricio and I said goodbye.

- You know, Isha, I don't think this is working out. Mauricio said.
- No, I don't think it is.

I got out of the car. I said goodbye to him.

That would be the last time I would see him.

I felt sad and relieved at the same time. It was sad for me to think that I had not been able to have a lasting relationship. The most I had ever been with someone was three weeks... with Mauricio. What was the matter with me? I was scared to let myself be carried away by sadness. I had experienced my father's depressive states second-hand, and just thinking that it could happen to me filled me with anguish. I blocked those feelings and felt temporarily relieved. "Too bad" I told myself.

The next week I was leaving for New Jersey to work as a babysitter for my cousin.

This would be the last year I would go help take care of her children during the summer.

Chapter 17

At home things were complicated. The economic situation gave me a feeling of anxiety combined with impotence. Let's say it was a tight economic situation for a middle class family. We had a roof to sleep under, thank God food was never missing and I had everything I needed in order to go to school. Of course, some luxuries were very restricted, like eating in restaurants, the clothes we were bought were from street markets, we had to use public transportation and there were practically no trips unless some friend invited me to her house in Cuernavaca. I am very lucky to have had all of that. I also had a mother who, despite her faults like any human being's, had the strength of an ox in order to support two teenagers: My brother and myself. It mustn't have been easy for her to give us permission to go out with our friends here and there. Having the responsibility of tending to her home as well as supporting it. She worked from sun to sun.

Mother, as is logical, liked us to wait up for her and sit up with her while she had supper because that was the hour when we could talk and be with each other even if it was only for a few minutes. At that hour my brother and I were like sleepwalkers. Our day had also started early, in my case at five thirty in the morning, and by eleven at night all I wanted was to do was go to sleep. It is incredible that in Mexico City for many families, as was my case back then, the time for family is from eleven to twelve at night! Of course during the weekends I hibernated. I couldn't get up. I was sleep deprived from the weekdays when I would only sleep five hours a night. In the mornings I had to get up at five thirty in order to catch the bus that took me to school at six. If for whatever reason I was late and got to the bus stop at six fifteen, I would probably not get to my first class, which was at seven, and not because it was far away from my school but because the buses that passed by would be so full of people that it was impossible to get on. On one desperate occasion I got on and hung to the frame of the door, but the first time the bus driver had to step on the brakes I almost went flying out. The public transportation system is terrible, so I either woke up early or I didn't get to school.

One night when my brother and I got home from the movies, we were scared by someone lying face down on our garden. My brother told me to stay by the garage door and not to move. He was going to see what was going on. The seconds seemed like hours. My heart beat harder and harder. In the middle of the darkness from where I was standing I couldn't see who it was.

- Papi? I heard my brother ask.
- Are you all right? Isha come… It's my dad, I don't know if something happened to him- he said in a worried voice.

I quickly ran to where they were. And yes, my father was lying in the middle of the yard, totally unconscious. The smell of alcohol was so strong that we immediately discarded any other hypothesis. It was not possible to move him. My father was a man that weighed more than one hundred kilos, so in that state it was not possible for us to put him anywhere else. Of course, he didn't care very much. We couldn't tell my mother what was happening because there was no phone at home and we didn't want her to get as scared as we had if for some reason she got home while we had gone to phone her. So we decided to wait in the garden. We couldn't do anything to wake my father up but I felt bad to even think about going in the house, get comfortable, and leave him lying there. A short while later my mother got home. We quickly went out to meet her and to explain the situation. With the lights of the car we were able to see a bit more. It was clear in that moment, the important thing was to light up the garden. My mother went over to look at him.

- Have you tried to wake him or something?
- Yes. We both answered. But he's not responding and he's too heavy to move.
- Well, my mother said, there is not much we can do, go in the house and bring a blanket so at least he won't catch a cold.

We went to get the blanket, we covered him up, and we went to sleep. I was not able to fall asleep. Sleep was uncomfortable for me given the situation, but of course my mother was right. What else could we do? Finally I went to sleep.

The next day I got up early for school and I went out to see how my father was. He wasn't there anymore. I went in the house, worried, but my mother told me in a soothing voice that he was asleep in her room. I didn't ask anything else. I went to school. That night my mother told us that my father had gone to Xalapa and that he would not come back to live with us again.

Inside, I felt a great relief. I didn't care that he had not said goodbye to us or that he had not given us an explanation. I felt like a weight had been lifted from my shoulders. My parents never lived together again. They only saw each other on two more occasions.

Little by little, my life followed its course. Sometimes I would feel like it was sunk in a deep, black abyss. My grandparents had lost their whole patrimony that they had taken such care of in order to have a peaceful retirement and paradoxically, now that they were old they were going through the most difficult economic situation they had ever gone through. My parents had gotten a divorce, my mother worked from sun to sun, my father was being consumed by alcohol in his room in Xalapa, and my brother had entered University. I was alone for the most part of the day. Now in the distance I realize that I was surrounded by blessings. The whole family had magnificent health, there was never food missing from the table, I went to school and I was about to finish high school.

The soap opera of my life had to come to an end.

If you want to make God laugh, tell him your plans. I had a plan. I was going to College to study Marketing and I had made up my mind to be one of the best students so that when I arrived at the seventh semester I could be a trainee in a transnational company, perhaps Procter & Gamble, Colgate, Coca Cola. After that, most likely I would get promoted within the company and I would be able to afford to rent an apartment with a friend and focus on work and be a great executive. Marriage was not a part of that plan, for the moment. Besides my relationships had not been very successful, so for the moment it was important to concentrate on other things.

Chapter 18

On August, 1991, I started College. The Mexico City campus was very small. They were just starting with the first and second semester of some careers, so there were few students. The only building that was finished was the pink one with the classrooms 1. On the ground floor there was a small cafeteria. In part of the first floor were the administrative offices and the teachers´ offices.

For me College environment was exciting and as I began my different classes I started to get to know a new, interesting world. Pablo Wydler was in four of the five subjects I coursed that semester. He was the boy I had met on the day of the admissions exam and that I had seen again when we had gone pick up the results. Now he was my classmate. He studied marketing too. His brother Charlie studied Industrial Engineering so I only saw him during breaks.

Little by little we became friends and one Friday Pablo told me:

- Hey Patty, a group of friends are going to go to the Bar Bar, do you want to come?
- Yes, sure, I just have to ask for permission. Why don't we call each other in the afternoon?
- Sure, I'll call you.

In those times, the first cell phones had come on the market. At home, after almost four years, there was still no phone. Telmex didn't have any lines for the area, so our only option for communication was a home cell phone offered by Iusacell. It was like a shoe-box which was the center, and it had a cordless phone. Calls were very expensive so we were instructed by my mother to be as quick as possible, that is, straight to the point. So my calls were telegraphic.

- Hello. How are you?
- What's up?
- I have permission. At what time are we meeting?
- Ok 7:30. Perfect. Bye.

End of conversation.

I invited my friend Karla to join us. At 7:30 Pablo picked us up at my house, and as we were going down the Picacho-Ajusco highway, he asked me:

-   Patty, do you mind if we stop to pick up my uncles?

Uncles? I thought. – Yes… of course, no problem- I answered.

I couldn't very well say no. I thought it was strange that his uncles would want to come with a group of teenagers, but it takes all kinds of people to make a world.

His uncles lived in San Jeronimo Lidice, in the street of Santiago, and to my surprise we were going in the house that was exactly in front of the house where I had lived in as a child. When we got out of the car to knock on the door I said to Pablo:

-   How odd, I lived right across the street!

A young, handsome, tall, thin guy looked out from one of the hallways and greeted us pleasantly and asked Pablo:

-   Where are you going?
-   We're going to the Bar Bar, why don't you come?
-   Well, let me just put on some shoes.

- That's my uncle Bernie. Pablo told me.

I didn't understand. How was it possible that Pablo had an UNCLE that young… and handsome? I was glad he was coming with us.

We arrived at the Bar Bar, we sat at a table to talk, listen to music and drink something. I, as was logical, only drank soda. That night I felt very lucky because Bernie sat next to me and we talked all night. Well, at least until eleven thirty because, as always, I had to get home and I knew how much my mother worried if I was a little late.

- Bernie, I'm sorry, but I have to get home.

Obviously, everyone else could go later, so I was cutting the night short for everyone. Bernie stood up and said something to Pablo.

- Patty, it's super early, call your mother and tell her you'll be a little longer. Pablo said to me.

On the inside I started to sweat. In the first place it wasn't so easy to find a phone in order to call home. Secondly I knew my mother didn't like me to do that. The agreement was that she gave me permission with the condition that I get home at the time we had agreed on.

And thirdly I could see everyone was happy and no one had the pressure of having to get home except for me. So I better get a phone because they way I was seeing things I wasn't going to get home on time anyway.

I saw one of the waiters and asked him:

- Excuse me, would you lend me your phone?
- No, miss. We don't lend it out. He answered.
- Please, I need to call home because I'm going to be a little late and my mother gets very worried, I really won't be long, it's just for letting her know.

Finally they unwillingly lent me their phone. I dialed and as I heard the ringing my heart sped up.

- Hello. My mother answered.
- Hello mami. It's me.
- What happened? By the tone of her voice I knew that there was no chance she would let me stay longer, but we still hadn't asked for the bill and I knew I had to let her know that I would be at least half an hour late.

- It's just that there are a lot of people and it's taking them very long to bring us the bill so I think I'm going to be like a half hour late.
- Why so much? My mother asked in an inquisitive voice, or at least that's how it felt to me.
- Well, I don't know. They already asked for it and we're on our way.
- All right, but just half an hour.
- Yes. I hung up. The time was upon me.
- What happened? Asked Bernie. You look worried.
- Yes, it's just that I have to get home and we still haven't even ordered the bill. My mother gets worried (and mad, I thought) if I'm late. I called her but she said I have to be home in half an hour.
- Don't worry, said Bernie. I'll tell Pablo now. The thing is he's the one with the car, if not I would gladly take you home now.
- Thank you.

Bernie went with Pablo. Finally they ordered the bill and we went home. We got there just in time. As we got out of the car I said goodbye to Pablo and Bernie and thanked them. Deep down I had the hope that Bernie would ask me for my phone number or something, but no. He said goodbye to me and my friend Karla and got back in the car. They waited for us to get inside and I heard the car start and drive away.

As I went in the house I heard my mother ask:

- Is that you, Isha?
- Yes mami, we're here, thank you.
- How was it?
- Very good, thank you. We're going to eat something and go to bed.

We went in the kitchen of the house to make ourselves something for supper and talk about the evening. While we made ourselves ham and cheese sandwiches Karla asked me:

- Hey, what did you think of Bernie? I saw you two talked all night.
- I liked him a lot and we had a great talk, but he didn't even ask for my phone number or when we could see each other again, nothing. I think he didn't like me. Too bad, because I liked him a lot.

We kept talking about this and that and went to bed. It had been a very interesting night.

Next Monday I saw Pablo in school and I didn't want him to notice how anxious I was to ask about Bernie.

- Hello Pablo, how are you?
- Good, what about you?
- Good, thank you... Well, I'm going to class.
- Yeah I'll see you later.

So nothing, he didn't say anything about Bernardo. I didn't dare ask. Besides, I couldn't very well say: Hey, did he say anything about me? Does he want my number by any chance? Something? Of course not! But this left me clueless, anxious, and unsettled. I couldn't concentrate on my classes. I took the rest of my classes of the day and went home. No news from Bernardo.

On Wednesday when I saw Pablo at school he finally asked me:

- Hey, I saw Bernie yesterday and he asked me for your number. Should I give it to him?

Should you give it to him! I thought

- Sure. I answered.
- Hey, and what did you think of him?

I thought he was handsome, nice, smart, pleasant. I thought.

- Well, really nice. I liked him. I said.

Luckily it was time for our next class. I didn't want to say anything more to Pablo and if he kept asking I would probably say more than I wanted to. I was so happy. He had asked for my number, maybe he had liked me also. Well, at least he had liked me as a friend. But it wasn't until Saturday that he called. When the phone rang I ran to it yelling: - I'll get it!!!!!

- Hello.
- Hello Patty. How are you?
- Very well, how are you?
- Good, thank you. What are you doing?
- Well, nothing (waiting for you to call), here in my house.
- Hey, what are you going to do this afternoon?
- Nothing special. The tic tic of the phone's taximeter ran quickly, I didn't want to cut him off and make him think I

was stuck up, but the call was taking too long.
- Do you want to go to the movies? My brother Rodrigo is also going with his girlfriend Diana.
- Yes, I have to ask for permission. Why don't you give me your phone and I'll call you back.
- I can wait if you want.
- No. It's just that this is a cell phone you're calling and it's expensive because they charge by the minute, that's why I'm talking so fast. I'll call you.

I was given permission. Rodrigo, Diana, and Bernardo picked me up. We went to the movies together to the Diana Theater that was in Reforma to see "The Homework". I liked the film a lot because it was an interesting proposal. The story was narrated through a still camara. The nudity scenes were a little uncomfortable for me, but I noticed everyone else was very relaxed so I tried to do the same, although I didn't achieve it. When the movie ended we walked along Reforma and later they took me home.

It was incredible, how well I got along with him. Finally I had found someone who I liked physically and whose personality I really liked too. Our talks always lasted hours and there were no awkward silences. There was so much to talk about.

We kept dating. Not as often as I would have liked, but we saw each other at least once a week.

In those long talks with him I found out that he was the eleventh of a family of twelve. Now I understood how he could be my friend Pablo's uncle. Pablo was the son of the eldest sister and Bernardo and Rodrigo were the youngest in the family.

One day he invited me to his house for dinner. His mother, who lived in Monterrey, was in the City and he wanted to introduce me. I, of course, was happy and terrified. The perfect moment for the end of the dream was the meeting with the "mother in law". He always spoke fondly of his mother and that comforted me.

We arrived at his house and some of his brothers and his mother were in the living room. What a surprise it was for me to find myself in front of this charming woman! With a smile on her lips she greeted me:

- Hello, you must be Patty. It's so nice to meet you!
- Hello. Likewise. It's very nice to meet you.

As always, I had failed to use the formal third person way of speaking we have in Mexico. Despite my efforts, there were people I simply could not use it with.

The conversation was very pleasant, I felt very happy. At Brando's house you felt free to be yourself, there was no need to pose or think twice about saying something or not, if you had to behave this way or that. It was simply about enjoying the moment, talking and spending time together.

It got later and later, one by one the brothers and sisters arrived until there were so many of them that I got them mixed up and I didn't know which was a brother, a wife, a son, or a nephew. It didn't matter, they were all charming.

Cinderella time came and I had to go home.

- Come on, stay a little longer. We just got here. One of them said.

- Yeah, we'll take you in a little while. Another said.

We had to leave... NOW! Because Bernardo didn't have a car so we had to walk in order to take a bus, then another one, and finally walk a few blocks to get there. This probably doesn't sound complicated but it took us an hour to get there. But we both did it happily.

I fell in love.

Chapter 19

My life at school was very pleasant, I had new friends and I was learning new things. I was very surprised by the technology they had at the Tec. I had a scholarship, so I had to carry out a scholarship service, which in my case consisted of helping a teacher digitalize students´ grades onto the system, register homework, and other things. What I liked most was when I had to pass things onto the computer. My first contact with one was at the Tec. In the offices of the teachers there were Mac computers. They were a kind of rectangular shoe box shaped and the novelty was that when you turned them on you didn't have to install the disquette with the Operative System, one entered directly into the system and graphically it was very friendly.

- Just don't click the wastepaper basket. Another classmate advised me.
- If you drag a document there, it will be erased and you won't be able to get it back.
- And remember to always save, because if you don't you'll lose the information.

- Yes. I answered and wrote down everything she told me so as not to forget.

These computers were amazing, you could do so many things.

At the Tec you also had the possibility of communicating with someone from the Tec at Monterrey. This area was very restricted and only the Informatics personnel had access to it, but one day in our computing class they gave us a demonstration.

The teacher sat in front of the computer and after a series of instructions, a message appeared:

- Hello, we are in Monterrey.
- Hello, answered the teacher. This is Computing I and we are teaching the students how to communicate between campuses.

I think that was the whole conversation. It was amazing. I didn't understand how they could have communicated. It was fantastic! Of course we're talking about January, 1992.

In College other worlds are opened to you. The contact with new information is fascinating. The subjects that had to do with math were hard, but I had the luck of having good teachers and good classmates that I studied with, although this didn't reduce my fear of taking the departmental exams. The teacher would let you know the date of when registrations would open in order for you to present your exam. I liked it when it was the first day at the first hour, that is, Monday at 7:00. That way I had the whole weekend to study. The exam was presented in a classroom and there we would sit, engineering students in one line, in another the Bachelor students. Besides, in front of you an accounting student would sit and behind you, an administration student. No one from your same Bachelor would be sitting anywhere near you. There were four different kinds of exams so in that way they made sure that there would be no copying.

Math exams were multiple choice. You had your exam, a blank page to make your exercises in, and the answer sheet, so in the answer sheet you had to circle the option that you considered correct. It seems easy to just guess the answer, but it was actually quite complicated because the answers were very similar and on some occasions the correct answer was that there was no correct answer and you had to explain why. The test caused me a lot of stress, but once I was done with it the rest of the tests seemed easy to me.

Chapter 20

When I was on the third semester of my Bachelor one day Bernardo invited me to go downtown because he wanted to show me where his father's office had been and the church were his parents had gotten married. The building where the office had been no longer existed because it had been damaged during the 1985 earthquake and they had had to tear it down. The Providencia Church was still standing, majestic. We walked in silence and sat on a bench. Each of us was in prayer. I crossed myself and heard Bernardo say:

- Patty, this is a very meaningful place for me because it is where my parents got married. That is why I want to ask you here: Will you marry me?
- Yes. I answered immediately with a smile on my face. Of course!

My answer was immediate. There was nothing to meditate. I knew that he was the man that I wanted to share my life with.

From his coat he pulled out a small black box, opened it and inside was a ring that he put on my ring finger. I felt more than happy. I felt radiant, glowing. I was so excited.

When I got to my mother's office she asked me:

- How did it go?
- Really well, I answered. Besides, I'm very happy because, look! – And I showed her my hand with the ring. Bernardo asked me to marry him.

She was speechless. It was logical. I think she never imagined that in that moment I would give her such news.

- But, have you thought it through? Why now? She asked.
- Well, because we love each other and I want to marry him.

Slowly my mother took in the news.

One day when we were walking back to my house at night Bernardo told me about the time when his father had gone with Francisco (his eldest brother) to ask his wife's hand in marriage to her parents house, and I said:

- I'm so sorry he is no longer with us! I would have liked it so much if he had asked for mine.
- Yes, so would I. He was a great person. He said.

Just as he finished his comment we started to hold hands and a bolt of electricity went though both of us and we let go of each other immediately.

- Ouuuch! I yelled.
- What was that? Bernardo asked.

It was as if a bolt of lightning had run through our hands. We were in the middle of the street. We shuddered. Somehow Brando's father was there with us, supporting us.

We had planned for our wedding to be very simple, at his mother's house in San Jerónimo. We had very little money and our budget was enough for some pizzas and sodas. It was fine. What we wanted was to be together and to share our happiness with those we loved

God's blessings are infinite. When we told Marcos (another brother of Brando's) and his wife Ceci that we were going to get married, they were thrilled. They were so excited that

Marcos immediately went to the computer and turned on Word to get started on the guest list. Ceci ran to her room and came back carrying her wedding dress. They had only been married for three months.

- Try it on! Ceci told me. And if it fits, you can wear it. Of course, if you like it.
- Of course I like it, I answered shyly.
- Go on, try it on.

It was incredible. The dress fit as if it had been made for me, perfectly. I didn't even have to turn the hem over or down. Ceci was my height and build. I just had to send it to the cleaners and that's all!

- Take it now. She told me. And let me get you the veil and the headpiece.

I didn't know how to thank them for so much help and solidarity. I was touched.

My father had been going through a very sober time in his life. I had gone to Xalapa with Bernardo, and to be able to talk to him a little made me very happy. I called him to tell him that we were getting married and he congratulated me and suggested that we get married in Xalapa and have the party at my grandmother's house.

Before we knew it, thanks to all the people who loved us, the wedding was arranged. We went from a pizza-garden celebration to a beautiful wedding with a wonderful celebration.

A week before getting married Bernardo asked me:

-   Patty, what is there going to be at the wedding?
-   I don't really know. I answered. The religious ceremony is going to be at the Fatima Church on Friday, September 18th and afterwards the party will be at my grandmother's house. I know that there will be white wine to toast with because my mother bought some and I think there will be something to eat to go with the toast. Oh, and I forgot! My aunt Charo is going to hire someone to play the organ so there will be music.
-   Great!

Chapter 21

We got married on Friday in Xalapa. My mother went to Xalapa before me in order to fix up the house and see to some details. We were going on Thursday afternoon because I had classes. On Thursday when I got to Brando's house in order to leave together, he told me:

- Listen, my brother Francisco called and asked me not to leave yet, to please wait an hour for him.
- Of course.

An hour passed and Francisco didn't arrive. Two hours and nothing. My mood started to change. I was getting married the next day. It was six in the afternoon and I wanted to get to Xalapa. We still had a five-hour trip ahead of us and Francisco was nowhere to be seen.

- What's the matter with Francisco? I asked, annoyed. It is six o'clock and we don't know where he is. I really want to go now. I was very serious.

- I don't know, but he asked us to wait for him.
- Yes, but he's not here and we're getting married tomorrow.
- Look, let's wait until seven. If he's not here by then I'll talk to him when we get back.
- All right, but at seven we're leaving.
- Yes, don't worry.

At six forty five, Francisco arrived.

- Hello, how are you?

To myself, I thought: Here… furious… waiting for you.

- Come here. He said. Come outside. There's something I want to show you.

Bernardo and I were in the living room so we went to the front door following Francisco. What a surprise when, in the garage, we saw a blue Volkswagen Sedan (Bochito, as we call them in Mexico) parked there with a huge red bow on the roof and the lights on.

- Congratulations! He said. This is Vero's and my gift.
- Fran… thank you so much…! Bernardo and I said at the same time.

- But… how incredible! This is great! Thank you so much! I can't believe it. I said.
- Get in. Let's go for a drive so you can try it out.

We got in and went for a short drive around the block.

- I wanted to give it to you today so you could take it to Xalapa.
- Thank you so much.

Finally we left with our friend Pablo Felix in his car. Our honeymoon was going to be in Veracruz, thanks to my brother who had given us three nights at a hotel, and we already had the plane tickets from Veracruz to Mexico. So the bochito stayed parked there, waiting for our return.

The drive was very peaceful, we ate all kinds of junk food on the way. We arrived late at night to Xalapa. My brother and I stayed at my grandmother's house, and Bernardo stayed at Arturo Marquez's house, a friend of his who also lived in Xalapa.

The next morning, the wedding day, we went to "La Parroquia" for breakfast, a very well-known restaurant where you usually order lechero, sweet bread and something else for breakfast. The conversation was very pleasant but I had decided to get a manicure for the first and only time in my life, I wanted to look nice on my wedding day and it was time to go the beauty parlor. So off I went.

I don't know if it was my nerves, my absent mindedness, or what it was but I felt like the lady at the beauty parlor was taking forever on the manicure. She went from one nail to another to another, it was three thirty and she didn't finish.

- Will it take much longer?
- No, I just have to paint the nails and then let them dry in order to give them another coat of paint.

What! Another coat. I'm getting married in three hours!

- I'm sorry, I said in the sweetest voice I could muster, but I'm a little short of time and I can't wait for a second coat.
- But, the pain won't last as long. She answered.
- Really, don't worry, one coat is fine.

I left the beauty parlor as quickly as I could. At my grandmother's house they had already eaten, so I ate some stuffed chiles in a kind of pickle sauce that I found on a plate. More like I gobbled them up. I felt the chile going down my throat in it's original shape. I drank some water so as not to choke. It was time to get ready. I did my own hair and makeup. I put on the wedding dress and went to find my father.

- Ready? He asked.
- Yes.

We headed towards the door to go down the half spiral staircase that led to the garage where the car was waiting, all fixed up. We were halfway down the stairs when I ran into Rodrigo.

- Where are you going? He asked.
- To the Church to get married. I answered.
- Oh God! I'm just arriving from Campeche and I didn't realize the time. I'll hurry up and meet you at the Church.
- That's a good idea.

The groom was so handsome. Seeing him, what was happening seemed incredible to me. Standing in front of the altar was Bernardo in his tuxedo waiting for me. The ceremony was lovely. They say that the choir sang beautifully, but I don't remember it. At the moment of presenting the coins, Mary and Pedro gave us two small trees of life... They have always liked being unconventional and they are very proud of Mexican crafts. When we saw these original "coins" Bernardo and I looked at each other without knowing what to say.

- I, Bernardo, with this tree of life that represents prosperity and eternal life... or something like that.
- I, Patty, with this tree, promise to take care of everything and... love you forever... or something like that.

They had said that they wanted something different from the accustomed coins but... plaster trees of life! We didn't even know what to say to each other. But the memory of those trees has given us many wonderful moments of laughter.

The mass ended, I offered my bouquet to the Virgin of Guadalupe, we got in the car and waited for a bit. They had told us that the bride and groom had to arrive at the party a little while after the guests. So the chauffer took us for a little drive around the city. When we considered that enough time had passed we went to my grandmother's house where the party would be. I think the drive was too long because when we got there, there was no place for us to sit. All the seats were taken. We were so happy to see how many people had come to our wedding. Family, friends, and of course friends of my parents, friends of my aunt Charo, and friends of my grandmother's who we didn't even know.

My mother quickly solved the problem. She got an aluminum table (one of the ones that Coca Cola used to give away for marketing reasons. She put a white tablecloth on it, some flowers, and the dishes and silverware. We shared that table with my cousin "El güero" and my nephew Esau who was also missing a seat. The food was delicious. My aunt Charo had ordered several typical dishes of Xalapa: Stuffed Xalapa style chiles, steak in plum sauce, chicken breasts in escabeche and I don't know how many other things, dishes I never saw but that people told me about afterwards, talking the wedding over. We have always been very grateful.

We danced, we talked, we laughed. We enjoyed our wedding very much. At night we decided it was time to go to the Port. We were very tired.

Our honeymoon was very nice. We rested and had new experiences. I felt very strange, not having to ask permission for this or that and especially from not having to call and let my mother know that we had arrived or something. I had the temptation to call my mother in the morning when we went down for breakfast. Next to the restaurant were some pay phones and when I saw them I had the impulse to and pick up the phone.

- What are you doing? Asked Bernardo.
- Umm… Nothing. I was about to call my mother and let her know we arrived and we're ok.

Bernardo looked at me in a way that made me understand that it was not a good idea and that I better not start calling my mother and letting her know about everything. I was married. I didn't need to call my mother all the time to let her know where I was.

I new stage of my life had begun.